DO talk to strangers

HOW TO **CONNECT** WITH ANYONE ANYWHERE

KERRIE PHIPPS
with JANE PELUSEY

CONTENTS

DO talk to strangers

Part 3: Resources, gratitude and connecting

TESTIMONIALS

"At last someone has said it: the test of whether we're serious about our human destiny as social creatures; the test of whether we even get what social capital is; the test of whether we know how to create a civil society is not how nice we are to family and friends, but how open we are to the needs of strangers. How else will they know that we take them seriously as fellow human beings?"

- Hugh Mackay, social researcher
and author of The Good Life and The Art of Belonging

"Do Talk To Strangers is an engaging and refreshing read, jam packed with valuable life lessons from cover to cover. With Kerrie's infectious enthusiasm, simple messaging and authentic use of real life examples, this book is a coaching aid like no other. It will enable you to learn more about yourself and give you the tools to connect; enabling you to gain a best friend, a mentor or simply unlock the doors to a fulfilling life journey."

- Kelly Howlett, Mayor of the Town of Port Hedland
and passionate environmentalist.

"The generosity, kindness and understanding that Kerrie's messages promote makes this book a must read for each and every one of us that hope for a more tolerant, peaceful world. I for one will now be more mindful of making the time to talk to strangers!"

- Rabia Siddique, Retired British Army Officer, Humanitarian,
Speaker and Author of Equal Justice

"This book is so relevant and essential for our time. Kerrie has a unique talent of demonstrating how much we may have forgotten or never realised, about the value of connecting with strangers. … when I travel, I find I connect more freely with strangers. Kerrie's words have been a sharp reminder of the need to bring the same to my everyday life."

- Justine Waddington, Founder, Encounter Travel,
Author, The Solo Traveller's Compass

"Insightful, engaging and a game-changer. In this book, Kerrie Phipps has given us a significant tool that we can use to boost joy, learning and success in our daily lives by nurturing new connections. Follow this book and see a whole new world unfold with every person that you meet. It all begins with taking that first step - talk to strangers."

- Jessica Sespene, Author of 7-Year Bliss,
How to Turn Your Deepest Pains Into Your Greatest Victories

"Kerrie's message and methodology is outstanding and she communicates it in an authentic and real way. I recommend her for any conference, training or coaching. This book will challenge your psychology and disrupt your thinking. It is one of the best books written for customer service and sales teams."

- Sam Cawthorn - Author of Bounce Forward,
Speaker, Philanthropist

"Kerrie's book is so delightful and refreshing in a busy world, where there is mistrust and skepticism of those that are different to ourselves. It is brilliantly written in the context of 'safety' but with such transparency and authenticity… to find so much 'hidden treasure' in those that enter and pass through our world. Knowing Kerrie for many years and her commitment to invest in others, she has become much richer for that life approach and as a psychologist I fully recommend this genuine, transparent and relationally enjoyable treasure."

- Ray Andrews PhD PACFA CAPA

"This book threatens to broaden your horizons and make you smile. In an age of indifference, loneliness and isolation, Kerrie Phipps encourages us to be truly human and to connect with each other. Her stories are real and radiate hope. As Kerrie suggests, a smile and a kind word can lead to so many possibilities."

- Hans Kunnen, Senior Economist
and Author of Borrow and Build

FOREWORD

There are a few favourite quotes that I love to remind myself of as I travel through daily life.

The first is something that emerged from reading thinker and author Edward de Bono:

To be interesting,
Be interested.

Life should not be boring when you realise that every person you wander by has a history, a heritage, a range of experience and, somewhere inside, a philosophy of life.

Every person has a story and something you can learn from.

For years I did a radio segment on the ABC in Western Australia called Thinking Caps. More recently this segment has been on Melbourne station 3AW with afternoon host Denis Walter. The gist of Thinking Caps is what we call Reverse Talkback.

In regular talkback radio, people ring in because there is a topic and they have an opinion to express on the topic. In Reverse Talkback we invite people to call in and they do not know what the topic is till we reveal it to them!

Our belief is that each caller will have some response to what we ask them and a story to tell. Often the response and story is uncovered with lots of laughter.

Reverse Talkback means our callers have to think on their feet. Or think in their mouths! And they do.

Everyone has a story.
Discover them.

A second favourite quote is a simple line from the American poet Walt Whitman:

I am large
I contain multitudes

Sometimes, with some folk, what you see is what you get. Often though, folk contain multitudes.

My Dad Jack was a craftsman, a carpenter; he worked as a sub contractor for decades. He was also a drummer who three times a week would be anchoring bands in pubs with his percussion. He also played clarinet. Oh, and banjo, piano, harmonica… the list goes on.

Dad was a quiet man who would come to life with music. (Or a beer. Or at a footy match.) His multitudes were there if you spent the time to discover them. They weren't splashed across social media and they weren't written on his forehead or spoken in his words. You unearthed them over time. If you were fortunate and a little bit curious.

Everyone has layers.
Revealed over time with care.

As a teen I started to see my Dad in layers and shades. We had moved from the red dirt of Kalgoorlie to the city of Perth and most weekends in winter I'd be playing footy and all other weekends I'd be at a beach.

I loved the simplicity of riding a wave as a body surfer. No board, just body. My mates were more board riders and, every now and then, we would all gather together to go to the Regal Theatre in Subiaco to watch a surf movie: waves, beaches, blonde haired girls… and music. In my mind the best of all the surf movies was *Morning Of The Earth* if only for its music.

One of the *Morning Of the Earth* tunes was titled *Open Up Your Heart* written and sung by G. Wayne Thomas:

There's no formula for happiness,
That's guaranteed to work
It all depends on how you treat your friends
And how much you've been hurt

But it's a start,
When you open up your heart and try not to hide,
What you feel insi-i-ide
Just open up your heart

It is my third quote to live by.

When it comes to on-going happiness; there is no formula. There is no recipe. However, there may be ingredients.

Some of these happiness ingredients are what you will find in this book. In order to grow our sense of humanity, in order to be enriched with learning, in order to extend our reach, we need to connect… with each other.

Everyone has possibility.
Find their wave.

Kerrie Phipps is a connector. Jane Pelusey is also a connector, a bridge bringing us the readers, together with Kerrie's thoughts.

Together, Kerrie and Jane's messages and methods bring us insights and ingredients to live with, to learn with and to lead a learning life through.

Once, in my years of back packing the World, I wandered into a remote youth hostel in the West of Ireland. On the wall was a plaque that said:

There are no strangers here, only future friends.

When we talk to strangers, we extend our ranges. When we read Kerrie's book we grow our web of life.

Enjoy.

Glenn Capelli
Speaker and author of *Thinking Caps*
www.glenncapelli.com

INTRODUCTION

Have you ever retraced your steps to remember how you arrived somewhere? To share with you how this book came about, and how it is that Jane Pelusey stepped in to help me gather my stories and pull teaching points out in a sensible order, I must retrace my steps.

I was invited to a charity breakfast with Sir Richard in 2010, which opened doors that have had a significant impact, which continues to this day and beyond. My Perth friend Terri Billington invited me to the breakfast. I met Terri in Melbourne with Dr Joanna Martin, who I was introduced to in an email from Shaun Stenning, who I met with Dale Beaumont.

I met Dale in 2007 after I read his book Secrets of Great Success Coaches Exposed and was so impressed with Dale's achievements at such a young age, I sent him a handmade, handwritten card of congratulations. He called me in response, and invited me to meet him for lunch when I was next in Sydney. At the time I was consulting for Results Coaching Systems (RCS), whose founder and CEO David Rock had written the foreword for Dale's book.

I connected with RCS and David through Google in 2004. Although I use Google quite often, every other connection I can think of has come through conversation – offline and online.

It's hard to imagine how my life and business might have unfolded if I hadn't written to Dale. He and his friends and mentors have contributed significantly to my personal and business development. There are so many inspiring people I've connected with since sending that card.

When you connect with a stranger, so many amazing doors can open.

If I hadn't said yes to lunch in Sydney… If I hadn't said yes to a breakfast in Perth, I would not have met Jane. What connections will you say yes to? What doors of opportunity will you open?

To retrace a little further, I must acknowledge my grandparents. My father's parents have passed away in the last few years in their late 90's and as I've always lived within an hours drive, their influence has been constant and appreciated. At their funerals people told me about how Bill and Jean Stockings made them so welcome when they first came to Gilgandra. Friendships developed that their descendants still benefit from today. My mothers parents, Violet and Garnett Tobin live in their own home in Sydney, aged 94 and 96 and they were always known for opening their home to the community, making people welcome and talking to people in the street. If you pass by when Grandad is mowing the lawn he'll be up for a chat.

When I took Grandad to Kokoda a couple of years ago he talked to every person he could, at the airport check-in, security, customs… you can imagine. He was so excited about his return to Papua New Guinea 70 years after his service there that he enrolled everyone around him in the joy of it. This is one of the easiest ways to connect with people. Go somewhere you're excited about, do something you're excited about and share the joy. It's contagious. It doesn't matter if you're more enthusiastic than anyone else. It might be confronting to some, but it will be so refreshing to many more.

A word from Jane Pelusey

Every time I catch up with Kerrie in person, I am fascinated about her ability to connect people. I have met people all around Australia through Kerrie and her "network". It seems like a natural gift.

The most interesting connections come from her ability to "Talk to Strangers" in a way that is so warm and enthusiastic that the stranger is immediately anything but a stranger anymore.

I personally use Kerrie as a mentor in this area and aspire to learn her amazing skill.

As an example, Kerrie and I were presenting at the Byron Bay Writers Festival. As we wandered around Kerrie chatted to people: festival attendees, festival volunteers and festival writers all equally and with authentic warmth and interest. I remember sitting in an audience with Tim Ferguson, Elizabeth Gorr, and Charlie Pickering on the panel. Kerrie's ability to "Talk to Strangers" meant that Charlie's girlfriend (who she had just spoken with in the greenroom) felt comfortable to sit with us. Because of Kerrie we became friends with many other talented authors during the event.

Kerrie's ability to connect also means she has extracted stories of "Talking with Strangers" from others. From each of these stories, both Kerrie's and from her networks, she has found lessons and learnings that can improve our lives and make the world a more friendly connected place.

Meeting Kerrie was pretty unlikely since she lived in Dubbo and I lived in Perth 3500 kilometres away. The wonders of social media broke the distance barrier. I saw a photo on Facebook with a fellow speaker friend Glenn Capelli and this woman who had written a book called Lifting the Lid on Quiet Achievers. In some ways

Kerrie's book had a connection to a series of books I was writing on living your passion so I went online and bought her book. Soon after I received a personal message from Kerrie introducing herself.

We started a conversation. She was coming to Perth to run a Conversations With Entrepreneurs event at a city bookshop. I asked if I could come along. That was my first Conversations event.

We interviewed Kerrie for our book series (which is mentioned further on in the book) and that just happened to be in Sydney. I think the next catch up was in Melbourne. We worked out we would be there in the same week, so we flew in two days earlier to meet up and attend Kerrie's Conversations event there. Connecting with people does require making an effort and being prepared to take action.

It may seem that we both travel to other locations to connect but we have both been to each others home towns a couple of times. We are interested in where our first international catch up will be as we continue a journey of Do Talk To Strangers.

We are so grateful that we connected. Jane has helped me realise that the connecting I do naturally is a skill that people want to learn and can learn. I'm always learning too, from every encounter with others. Learning occurs when I take a moment to reflect on the conversation. This book helps you reflect on your connecting.

Who are you so grateful that you connected with? When you consider your relationships, you'll see that the people you know have:

• always been there
• were introduced to you by a mutual friend or acquaintance

- introduced themselves to you, or
- you introduced yourself.

These last two are the opportunities that could easily have been missed, but someone had the confidence to talk to a stranger, which most of us were warned not to do when we were children. It's a natural activity for the brain to assess a stranger as either 'friend' or 'foe'. Far too often, the brain makes the incorrect assumption that a stranger is a foe. At the Neuroleadership Summit in 2013, neuroscientist Jessica Payne shared evidence of how a blank or neutral expression is read as a threat.

Are you willing to be open to the idea that strangers could actually be friends you haven't met yet?

Perhaps you've made that decision, and you are the person who smiles at everyone in the street, waves and says hello. If you are this person, then you know what an exciting adventure it is to meet people. Attendees of conferences I've spoken at often send me messages in the weeks that follow about how they've made a conscious choice to be open to make eye contact, smile and say hello to people, and they're finding it surprisingly easy and rewarding. "It really enriches my day – and theirs", they report.

If you wonder how could people possibly connect with total strangers, if you're curious about this, then you might just find this book a life-changer. If you're thinking, "I always talk to strangers – I could have written this book", please enjoy the journey here as you relate to our adventures. Also please write and tell me your own adventures or join the conversation on social media (#DoTalkToStrangers) and continue to encourage others.

Let's go!

You might be looking for a book to help you connect with people so that you can further your career and business. Read on and this will help you significantly, but I'm asking you to put aside your specific business goals for the moment and take a closer look at your thinking and your attitude towards others. Maybe you'll find that your goals fit beautifully with what you're reading. However, letting go of being attached to an outcome brings surprising results.

Let's take a deeper look into what goes on in the creating and building of connections and discover a whole new world opening up. It's about participating in great conversations, the adventures that unfold and the connection between human beings that is possible when we take a chance. We'll go behind the scenes, and look closely at what happens before you even set eyes on a stranger who could become your friend, colleague, mentor or client.

There are many books and events about how to network for business, how to impress people, and how to make people buy from you. This book and my events aren't typical business networking. It's natural to think "What's in it for me?" but please don't let that be the first thing that comes out of your mouth. I've heard people say this, and it's an immediate 'disconnector'. When this intention is ahead of serving others it's a filter that actually blocks your sense of possibilities. I believe that the best way to connect with anyone, whether for business or friendship, is to present them with yourself, the real you, the curious you, the authentic you, with your attention fully on them, listening without thinking of what to say next, being in the moment and open. It's about an attitude of service – how can I serve this person? It's being open to what is possible. Which may turn out to be a big win for you, for them, or for someone else, and it will be joy.

There's a world of difference between an attitude of "What's in it for me?", or an intention to connect for your own agenda, and one of genuinely caring, being interested in people with a heart to serve others and make a difference. It's servant leadership. This isn't servitude or being a doormat, but something the best leaders understand. Leading by example, thinking of others, hearing what they're saying. Listening in a way that is a gift to others as well as yourself. You can learn to be a great listener. You can rediscover your innate curiosity and your authentic self.

We begin life curious, open and expressive. Babies cry and laugh freely. They grow up and become shaped by the opinions and judgements of those around them – "Do this, don't do that, be quiet, speak up, have a go, don't be silly, don't talk to strangers, play it safe". Oh, and this classic – "Contain yourself!" Have you ever been a little 'too' excited, joyful or expressive in a way that has made others uncomfortable? It's just that they don't relate, they don't share the joy – but that doesn't mean you have to always dampen it. If we do contain ourselves, we are literally putting a lid on our joy, our creativity and expression, and we screw the lid on tight. And become uptight. No longer free. Sound familiar?

What takes up most of your thoughts? Is it making things happen, getting things done, adding more items to your list, and not enough ticks of accomplishment? So much busy-ness gets in the way of connecting with others, which could make all the difference in the world.

This book comes in three parts:

- the first part goes through my model of how to talk to strangers and connect with people
- the second part is how to apply this in any scenario, with anyone, anywhere

- the third part includes resources to continue your learning and sharing.

I have many stories of the rewards of talking to strangers – some have become friends, associates, clients and mentors. Some have opened a door of opportunity for me, which generally opens doors for others, and some are people I've been able to connect with others who can support them or they can receive support from. People come into your life sometimes just for a moment, and sometimes for a lifetime.

I hope that as you read this book you'll turn some of my tips and your ideas into actions, and that your insights will not only change the way you see the world, and increase the ease with which you connect with strangers, but it will connect you more powerfully where it really counts – those nearest and dearest.

PART ONE

Do talk to strangers

MY CONFESSION

Anyone can talk to strangers. We all do from time to time, often without thinking about it, and not just 'talk' but 'listen' and 'connect'. Sometimes it's when we feel completely safe to do so. Many times we take a risk – the most common risks are rejection or misunderstanding. I'm asked quite often, "But how do you talk to strangers, Kerrie? How do you start a conversation with a completely random person?" There's an assumption that I'm just really confident, but I have not always connected naturally. Perhaps I did when I was a young child, like most children in safe environments. Life and its events beat the confidence out of me for many years, so I keep restoring it and growing it. I just put myself out of my comfort zone and am happy to be uncomfortable just to give things a go.

Whether it's new food or having a go at something that I haven't done before, it's just applying that sense of adventure and sense of "You know what? I'm just going to do it. I do love to connect with people". Of course I'm not always happy to be uncomfortable. Friends and family have challenged me from time to time when they've seen me hesitate. They remind me that I get out of my comfort zone in other ways, so why would I turn down the opportunity to try something new? Simple things, like olives, I thought I'd hate but now appreciate along with mushrooms, oysters and octopus.

When did I start talking to strangers? Okay, here's where I have a confession to make …

My life in Dubbo began at 17 (well actually at 16 when I ran away from home with a crazy bad attitude – another story altogether). The black sheep of the family returned home about five weeks later and remained on my parent's farm. I studied at Gilgandra TAFE College for the next 12 months until I began working in a dental surgery in Dubbo, where

I had no friends. At least none who wanted to go to the nightclubs with an underage farm girl on Thursday, Friday and Saturday nights. If I had no-one to meet up with, I just pretended that I did.

I was completely alone, sitting at a table, glancing at my watch every now and then, looking at the door, and around at other tables. Once I'd made eye contact (and smiled) a couple of times, I'd casually approach another table and say hello, and ask did they mind if I joined them as my friends hadn't arrived yet. Of course people were welcoming. After all, everyone knew what it was like to have friends running late, and being the first one to arrive anywhere, especially in the days when mobile phones were a big box in the back of a car. One of the best friends I remember meeting this way was a young man in the airforce. He had a girlfriend back home and was loyal to her, so I really appreciated making a friend who didn't change his intentions towards me, and he happily introduced me to many others at the RAAF base in South Dubbo.

Please hear me, it's not my advice to be fake. I've dropped that approach a long time ago, but I haven't dropped the habit of meeting strangers. Now I just tell the truth. It's just easier! While in confession mode, I'm reminded of another night back then when I faked something else ... a fiancé. I'd noticed that young men were not all going to the nightclubs just to make friends, as I was, so I decided a little tool would help me keep relationships purely platonic. I wore a very inexpensive ring that looked like a gorgeous big diamond solitaire engagement ring and invented a fiancé who worked out of town. This worked well for a couple of weeks till I went out without it and some of my new friends knew that I was single. A very upset young man yelled at me one night saying, "I wanted to hit on to you last week but I thought you were engaged!" A compliment perhaps, but not very romantic!

Although it might seem rather confident to go out alone and make new friends (some are still friends 21 years later and know the real me) I was not confident at all. My desire to be accepted and to be with people was greater than my insecurity and lack of confidence. I am still, and will always be, a people person. I love getting to know people, and at the time I pretended to be confident in order to connect. When your desire to connect is greater than your fear of rejection, your world expands beautifully. With the following question you can explore how you can minimise awkward moments and connect confidently. Consider how you already get out of your comfort zone with a physical or mental stretch, new foods, places, people, sports, education …

COACHING CORNER

Ask yourself:

- In what ways do you get out of your comfort zone?
- By acknowledging your bravery in that aspect of your life, you can transfer your bravery to another.
- So now that you've noticed other steps you've taken, what's your next step out of that comfort zone?

Consider your wins and apply the learning.
Fill in the gaps with your accomplishments:

Remember the times I was out of the comfort zone and achieved

....

....

so I'm more courageous than I've given myself credit for. I can talk to anyone! This week I'd like to

....

....

 Start - *rather than waiting until you're confident – just have a go!*
Notice *what went well and revel in the smiles you gave and received.*

THE 'ASKING' MODEL

There are six essential components that make up the skill base behind how to really cultivate this skill that can seem almost like magic. I share this in the framework of ASKING.

You know it's true from experience that many times 'you have not because you ask not' – so let's have a closer look at asking. You have to 'ask' or gain permission to have a conversation anywhere. People are often closed off to conversations or connecting because their brain is engaged elsewhere. We don't know what is going on in another person's world, so we need to give people an opportunity to shift gears in their thinking and refocus. This is the essence of permission – it's not merely being polite – it's engaging another person's brain and giving them a chance to respond.

Permission is the fastest way to connect with people and there are so many ways to 'ask'. It might even be a questioning look – WITH A SMILE – and making eye contact. In a noisy environment there may be no need for words, but making eye contact with someone and smiling and glancing at the space you'd like to squeeze into could be all that's needed for them to be open to welcoming you.

To enter someone's space you either ask permission or you are given permission. It's only 'their space' because they were there before you, for example, a waiting room or a train. When entering a train there might be one space available to sit down. It is an empty seat so you have a right to it. You are approaching people so make eye contact if you can, although they are sometimes engrossed in a magazine or a phone. There's often an unconscious permission given or you can just squeeze in there and stare at the floor. It is very subtle but makes a huge difference.

There is an opportunity to ask permission such as "do you mind if I sit here?" It is not necessary but is a great opportunity to connect when you have to sit next to a stranger. You can just wriggle in there, or do it with a smile and make eye contact, which will make you and everyone else around you more comfortable to have further conversation if the opportunity arises. If you are the person already sitting, you have an opportunity to connect, by smiling and making room. You connect because you feel there is permission to or because you create the sense of permission for the other person.

We are so fearful of rejection. To engage someone's brain, you require permission with the simplest question. It doesn't mean saying "Can I have permission?" It is much more subtle than that. You will see examples of permission throughout the book. Even in some of my questions, I am asking permission to think these concepts through. Permission is not a one-time done deal for communication, unlike a school permission note. When we are talking to others, we are gaining permission for a deeper level of communication and connection. It is one level to ask the time of day, but another to ask about someone's family. The ASKING model is not just a cool acronym. It is about asking questions, about asking permission, little by little increasing the connection with other human beings.

We influence and affect each other so much more than we realise. Scientists can demonstrate through all kinds of testing that suppressing emotion affects those around them to the point of raising another person's blood pressure. But you probably knew that – you've felt it, at least subconsciously. Have you ever asked someone "Are you okay?" and they say "Yes I'm fine" – but you feel like something is not quite right. And of course you can think of times you've thought someone was down but they were focused, didn't see you, then broke into a big smile when they caught your eye. You feel relieved and happy, influenced by a momentary connection.

To notice how easily you're influenced by others, think about how you felt last time you saw a policeman in uniform, or someone in a car behind you blasted their horn, or when you saw a child skipping down the street. All of these people can be complete strangers, yet their appearance, behaviour or demeanour can influence you in a split second, sending you into a stressed state or putting a smile on your face.

Awareness

We don't make significant progress with any goal without a good awareness of the situation. In terms of talking to strangers (or anyone you want to connect with) we need to be more aware of them. It's so important to increase your self-awareness too. How are you responding or reacting to those around you? How can you focus on others and serving them, while not losing your sense of self, but becoming more self-aware and others-aware.

I believe that people are important, whoever they are. It's not all about me and what's going on in my head. I can get caught up in thinking about what I need to be doing. Everyone else has stuff going on for them too. When I look beyond myself to focus on and help others, the answers and help I need usually appear anyway. I can ask for help too. I've learned this from challenges I have faced and through helping others. When you give to other people, you do so because you want to and choose to.

Being self-aware and others-aware, self-focused or others-focused, is not a balance thing or an either/or thing. There's no perfect sweet spot that fits every scenario. For example, when someone dives into an icy raging river to save a child, they are completely focused on another and aware of their situation. Their own self-interest is forgotten in that moment, but of course not forever. The extreme situations aren't sustainable.

Being focused entirely on yourself and your goals will cause your network to diminish rapidly. People refer to a 'self-made millionaire' but I wonder how there can be such a thing. They may see themselves (or be seen) as very independent, but surely they had parents – present or absent – who had an impact that was positive or negative that could have contributed to their success. They had customers of some kind, whether the relationship was good or not. We can't do life without other people – and if we connect well we make it easier on everyone!

"A man wrapped up in himself makes a very small package"
– Benjamin Franklin

If you're aware of yourself and what's going on for you, you could be focused on what you want and/or need to get done, but you may not be as others-aware as you could be. Or you may think "it's not all about me" and turn the tap off to your own life. We can try to fill our own life but then not know when to give. Similarly if someone wants to give to you don't be a martyr. Accept the offering.

Assess: How's your self awareness?

Do you know yourself, what lights you up and energises you? What drains you? Do you know what it is to 'listen to your body'? When I was told in 2003 by Dr Ray Andrews (psychologist and friend) to listen to my body I was in a deep dark hole of burnout, and so focused on getting stuff done and 'helping others' that I didn't have the self-awareness (clearly in denial and 'too busy') to recognise that I was very unwell. Until he said that, I hadn't seen – or I'd ignored – the warning signs of extreme stress; stomach cramps, tightness in the chest, insomnia and thinking through to-do lists at 3am. When I became aware of these symptoms I could make the necessary changes and recover my health. There are so many checklists and tests available through doctors, other health practitioners and coaches and they all can be useful in raising your awareness. Check out the resources at www.kerriephipps.com for support in these areas.

How's your others-awareness?

Do you expect others to be like you, think like you, want what you want – or do you recognise that every person is unique? The maps of networks in every brain are different, just as every map of every city in the world is unique. Do you see people as you pass them by? Do you see opportunities to make eye contact and smile? Do you know that people ask themselves sometimes, "Do I matter?", "Does anyone know I exist?" or "Do they care?"

Being aware of others is not only kind and respectful, it's essential for making the world a brighter place. The essence of this book is AWARENESS – OF SELF AND OTHERS – and the journey we'll take together though these pages will raise your awareness and your world will enlarge in a beautiful way.

Being present is about awareness-of-self-and-others. I think I would have called myself others-aware, but see now that I wasn't really. I may have been 'others-focused', but I was still on autopilot, responding and reacting to what I saw on the surface. That is, hearing what people said, or what I thought they said, and not really being present and hearing between the lines. Not hearing the 'still small voice' within me.

Being present means not being anywhere else in your thinking, not being on autopilot, and thinking about the other things going on in our lives. When on autopilot, you may think you are present, but you are not thinking about anything else. You are not thinking of others or yourself on a more conscious level. Being present is a practice of slowing down, taking notice of what is going on within and around you.

There are many networking events in any major town or city you could attend. You might observe people in suits looking altogether professional, polished, and sometimes pretentious, and be daunted. But there is a real person underneath and that is who you want to connect with. The networker's intention might be to gather and give out lots of business cards and be remembered for being the most impressive. People can seem full of their own importance and desperation for more clients and another sale. This does sneak through in unconscious ways and may be glaringly obvious to others, despite the efforts to cover it up. You can't judge someone else's intention, or know exactly why you sense the vibe that you do, but you can choose your own intention and let go of the pressures that may drive you.

For example, if you're going to a function and are desperate for a sale you will drive people away from you. I'm sure you've been on the other end of someone's desperation and it's not nice. You draw back. But you've done business with people who've been there for you, hearing what you want. Be the listener, the one who is focused on others – you won't go without. Know what you're passionate about, what you're good at, and how you can serve others, and your opportunity to make your sale will come.

If you're caught up in a sense of desperation - let's be honest, anyone in business or employed to make sales has felt this at some point - notice it, let it go. Even if you have to talk it out with a coach or mentor, write it down, screw up the paper, and let it go physically and mentally and walk in with a clear, positive, service-focused intention.

Why have you connected with some of the people you have? Think about what reasons you have to connect with people? Think about the last 24 to 48 hours. Have you connected with people, and what was your reason for doing so? If you're struggling to recall a recent encounter, think about your last holiday or weekend trip when you were away from home, more relaxed perhaps. Who did you connect with? Sometimes it isn't to get anything. You might not have purposefully been compassionate or wanting to give, but you just brightened someone's day. You simply connected, and it was not difficult, so it was probably an intuitive response. You were being present, in the moment, not feeling nervous.

Some of the reasons for connection can be about getting more information. It could be for people in business or just looking to help others. Your reason might be to gain a new client or to expand your network. It could just be for the joy of connecting or the joy of learning.

However, when you're really attached to specific reasons for connecting you lose the joy of it and I see this at almost every business event. When you carry the joy of connecting into a business scenario you open more doors for yourself and others. Often, we put so much pressure on ourselves. If you are going to a business event and you want to promote your business, there is added pressure, so choose another reason. Decide you are going to connect with people tonight because you just want to get better at connecting. You might want to express an interest in people. You might want to enjoy yourself. You want to take the pressure off and just connect and be present.

Make a list of your own reasons for connecting with people you come by. Then come up with a list of other reasons to connect with people but were possibly too afraid to try. If you might have thought, "Yes, I don't really talk to people in shops because I want to get in and get out", then you might connect with curiosity in other places or you might connect with caring or wanting to lift someone's day,

When you make your list of reasons to connect, make two columns. List the reasons that you currently have for connecting. It doesn't matter if it's business, or managing boredom, just passing the time, or anything. Write down the reasons that you actually do connect for and then, in the other column, the possible reasons that you could have. We can choose to be curious, or to learn more, or to be more adventurous, or to be more focused and more intentional. You might find yourself connecting in ways that get you stuck in a lengthy conversation that you don't really have time to be in. That conversation is a few pages on from here for people who ask – How do we 'get rid of people' in a respectful way? How can you connect in a way that is respectful and yet succinct?

Everyone's lists are going to look different, and as you look at yours, be aware of the conversation in your head and the reasons that you connect. Explore your thinking with curiosity, not judgement.

COACHING CORNER

I currently connect:

- To ask directions
- To check the time
- To pay a compliment
- To grow my business/network

I could also connect...

- To share the joy of something, such as a gorgeous day!
- To find and give a sense of connection
- To encourage someone
- To put a smile on someone's face

Choosing your focus everyday is helpful in the process of talking to strangers. It is very easy to put your head down, busy yourself, and not to talk to strangers, but you are missing out on a world of amazing connection and experiences.

Actually I had a moment of being so focused recently that I didn't connect as well as I could have. I was focused on finding a restaurant recently at the Opera House in Sydney and I walked right around to the far end (as Google maps told me that our destination was right up there), conscious that my husband Lyndon and his mum were following me at a distance. As I passed a number of offices at the back of the Opera House I came across two young men sitting in the dark against the wall, and it didn't seem that there were any public entrances. I assumed they might have worked there and popped out for a break.

Instead of breaking the ice and gaining permission with something like "Hello! Can I ask ...", I simply said "Do you happen to know your way around here?" I didn't get much of a response from the one nearest, but the other stood up and asked what I was looking for and was helpful in suggesting where the restaurant might be. It ended well because I was immediately aware that my approach could have been more relaxed and friendly, so I changed my tone, expressed my gratitude, and wished them a great night.

There's always an opportunity for learning! If you notice that you've rushed into a conversation with stress or uncertainty and set the tone with it, it's never too late to pause, shift gears, and take the conversation to a more relaxed, lighter or happier space. And be open about it. If you say "Sorry, I've been rushing. Can I start again?" you'll probably find the other person more interested in you, leaning towards you with empathy rather than leaning away.

Notice your energy. If you're stressed, tired, cranky or worried, people aren't as likely to engage with you – unless their 'empathy radar' is on. Learn to choose your focus, your attitude and shift your energy. A positive energy will bring walls down, sometimes in practical ways like people offering you their place in line, or giving you an upgrade or other acts of kindness. Really, if you worked in a hotel would you want to make someone's day when they're rude to you compared to someone who is friendly and energised? Unless you're on a mission to lift someone's spirits, you might amplify the positive energy of others. Or let the energy of others amplify your own.

A great way of increasing your self-awareness is to notice the conversation in your head. The first time I became aware of this concept was when my colleague Mary Britton from New Zealand asked me, "What was the conversation in your head at that moment?" The moment she was referring to was about half an hour earlier when I was supporting her in a training room with new coaches. I felt that I'd let her down by not being as concise as I could have when she and I were demonstrating a succinct conversation. As she asked me the question, I reflected and realised that the conversation in my head was one of self-criticism. In fact, I'd spent the next 10 minutes until the coffee break beating myself up in my head about how I could have and should have done better.

You might be familiar with this internal conversation of "Why didn't I say..." or "I should have said ...". This kind of conversation takes you right out of the present moment, keeping you stuck in the past, or thinking about your future conversations and how you might be able to redeem yourself in the eyes of others. Once Mary highlighted my thinking – increased my awareness – I was able to let go of the unhelpful 'conversation in my head' and be focused in the present moment.

I've since met Dr Daniel Siegel, author of *Mindsight: The New Science of Personal Transformation*, at Neuroleadership Summits and learned more about noticing and changing the conversation in my head. There are so many neuroscience books available now about the social brain and what's happening when we're making connections with others. Neuroscience is a fascinating field that informs the way we interact, how we connect and disconnect, how we make decisions, and the conversations that we have, so I've listed more great resources at the back for further reference.

Start small ... smile and scare yourself a little

Once you have made the decision to talk to a stranger or connect with someone who you may have thought about, and you've chosen your focus, the next step is to connect. The initial connection is very small. It can be a matter of eye contact, then a smile, and say hello. There it is – the three steps to connect:

• Make eye contact
• Smile
• Say hello

And if this is terrifying – scare yourself in a small way. A tiny but significant way…

Develop your curiosity and awareness of the world around you

This is easily done, and is so rewarding. Step outside, perhaps go for a short walk, and pay attention to the world around you. Look at the colours, search out your favourite ones, and notice similarities and differences. Look for the beauty in your environment. If you are looking for beauty, creativity and uniqueness, you'll shift your brain into a more positive, engaged state where you literally become clearer in your thinking and more creative and happier.

When you notice colours, shapes and things that you like, you'll see things about people that you like. You'll notice a pleasant demeanour, a lighthearted walk, a ready smile. (By this I mean a pleasant face that may not be smiling, but there's a smile ready to emerge as you make eye contact.) You'll notice colours on people – you might even feel like saying "Oh that's a lovely colour".

The three connection points above are not set in stone. Connections can happen in many ways.

One way to find connection points is paying compliments such as:

- "Hi, just wanted to say I love your earrings – I have similar ones and love wearing them".
- "Cool shoes!"
- "That's a great suitcase, where did you find that?"
- "You were thinking ahead about the weather, bringing such a great jacket".
- "Can I ask you where you got such a unique piece?" (luggage, jewellery, clothing)
- "You seem to know your way around – can I ask you a couple of questions?"
- I've often asked "Do you know the area?" or "Are you a local?"

For people who just want to connect better, whether it's for business or whatever reason, practice. We can make someone's day in the meantime, while you're practising connecting with people. Notice interactions at checkouts, on trains, in taxis. Notice how much eye contact there is. See how many people you can make eye contact with. If you are going to look someone in the eye, be relaxed and have a smile. Be the first one to smile. Without eye contact you will not pick up on so many cues such as whether they are relaxed, intimidated or preoccupied.

It's important to be okay with an awkward moment. It doesn't mean you lack intelligence or aren't socially savvy enough. It just means you're having a go. The important thing is to let go of pretense. It's really not helpful to anyone to silently be trying to look cool. You'll look uncool. If instead you say, "I feel a bit awkward asking this" or "I wondered if I can ask you about such and such", you could get a very different response. If you confess to feeling a little awkward or nervous, the person you're talking to will want to put you at ease. They may well

say, "Oh that's okay, please ask" or "No, don't be nervous!"
Notice public speakers, especially new ones. There's nothing wrong
with someone confessing to start with that they feel nervous. It actually
connects them to the audience, as many people in it will be glad that it's
not them up there!

At the Neuroleadership Summit in San Francisco we heard from the
Human Resources executive of Twitter, Janet Van Huysse. One of her
opening statements was that she was nervous, as this was her first time
speaking at a conference like this. She then went on to deliver a brilliant
presentation, in tandem with neuroscientist Carol Dweck. What she
did by expressing her nerves was actually let them go. If she'd tried to
hide them in order to 'look professional' we would have felt (consciously
or unconsciously) that she wasn't being completely authentic and we
wouldn't have been so engaged in the presentation. She came across as
very professional and with great credibility anyway! Many of us went
to talk to her after the session to acknowledge her presentation and I'm
sure she went home encouraged and more confident about speaking.

The fear of awkward moments

The fear of awkward moments stops so many conversations that could
be truly amazing. Here's a few that might stop you from engaging with
others. It's really fear of rejection, fear of what others think... let it go!

"Fear is going to be a player in your life but you get to decide how much"
- Jim Carrey

What if they don't look at me, or just glance and look away?

Don't take it personally – they'll have things on their mind that have
nothing to do with you. Feel free to leave them be. Your brain might be
telling you that it's your fault, that you're not worthy of a conversation,

that you don't matter – but that's just your brain's default setting to warn you of danger. It's not actual danger, so thank your brain for watching out for you and tell it that it's overreacting. Get on with your day and find someone else to smile at. And they may not even be ignoring you – if they're preoccupied they didn't even see you, even if they appeared to be looking at you!

What if I say something stupid and look like a complete idiot?

Ah, we've all had these moments. We expect perfection of ourselves and let others off the hook saying, "You're only human!" We're all going to have moments of being vague, saying something inappropriate or irrelevant, and feeling the sense of disconnect. I still do. The important thing is to be able to let it go. Don't beat yourself up for it as that will only inhibit clear thinking even more.

What if I have no idea what to say in the first place?

Perhaps there's no need to say anything, but if you want to connect, if you sense that you like this person, or that they have an answer to something you need or want, just step out and say something. I did this one day when I had noticed a tall, elegant redhead at a conference and didn't know what to say, but wanted to make a connection with her.

In a crowd of 20,000 people at Hillsong Conference at Olympic Park in Sydney she stood out to me. I had nothing intelligent to say but I caught up with her as she was walking to a bus and said, "Hello! I just wanted to meet you" (feeling a little sheepish). Then I said, "I'm Kerrie, I'm from Dubbo". She replied, "Oh my goodness! Perfect timing – my friend Paula is moving to Dubbo next week and doesn't know anyone!" This was the start of a beautiful friendship with Paula and my family. Lucinda, the beautiful redhead I wanted to meet, was the connector. Perhaps a simple hello is more intelligent than we assume.

How do we 'get rid of people' in a respectful way?

We need to have boundaries. A boundary might be a limit you put on your time and energy, simply by being clear on what your focus is. I think people forget that they can say, "No thank you". You are not compelled to stay in a conversation, to buy something or commit to anything. You can excuse yourself respectfully. It's okay to say, "I need to close my eyes for a while, I've had a big day. Will you excuse me?" It will leave the other person feeling good, not like they've been a bother if you can acknowledge or thank them for something.

Perhaps it would be relevant to say, "So nice to hear about your family, thank you for telling me about them. Would you excuse me? I need to collect my thoughts about a presentation I am giving soon". Be honest, because if you get caught out you will make them feel insulted – and no-one likes to feel deceived.

I can remember someone being caught out many years ago when not very many people had mobile phones. A business man was standing in line at the bank appearing to have a conversation on his mobile, when suddenly his mobile phone rang, revealing his dishonesty. Oh cringe! Now we can only guess why he may have been pretending to be on a call as he walked into the bank, but I can tell you that public opinion dropped in that moment. If he's pretending to be on the phone, in what other aspects of business is he pretending?

Be respectful and understand that not everyone is like you, whether you are the chatterbox or the listener, and no-one thinks exactly as you do or sees the world as you do.

Suspicions

When a stranger speaks to you, your natural tendency might be to be suspicious. It could be your intuition, noticing whether or not you are in a safe place. Many public places such as malls, hospitals and universities have security guards. It is okay to ask them to walk you to your car or share any concerns you have. The small chance something could go wrong can keep you from so many amazing adventures. Fear of falling off playground equipment can impact on a child, and fear of rejection can deprive you of not only fun, but valuable, learning experiences.

Even if you don't have much energy or time to connect, start small. Take a few minutes, once a day or once a week, if you want to start smaller! Be open to connect with someone.

Keep going with quality questions

This is not about learning a list of quality questions – people sense your heart and the attitude you ask in. So let's look at the heart and science of quality questions, because whether you're on a train or a plane and you want to have more connections with people, consider how you actually do that. How do you ask questions that don't seem confronting or invasive? I was thinking about a couple of blokes that I was working with who wanted to be better connected in both life and business. However they worry about being judged as trying to pick up women when they simply want to connect and get to know more people.

I could be talking to someone my age or younger, perhaps a man on a train, and you might think that I'm 'hitting on to him' or 'making advances', but I know I'm not. I'm happily married and love meeting new people, but strangers don't know that. How do you have a conversation and ask questions and engage someone without them thinking there's an ulterior motive? How do you have a lovely stranger-to-stranger connection without being judged? We can prepare for that, but we can't always know how it's going to go. People have their own frame of reference and might decide that anyone who talks to them has ulterior motives. You might be able to turn that around with some great questions that create a positive response.

It's also about being acknowledged as another human being, just to be seen and noticed. It really can make quite a phenomenal difference. All that happens when we get ourselves out of our own way. That's when we have the powerful conversations, powerful connections.

Many people are uncomfortable about walking into a room where there are groups of people already chatting to each other. You walk in on your own and you think, "Which group am I going to go to?" What do you say when you get into the group? Make eye contact with someone and smile. Be ready to listen. Then the attention is not on you. It's on them. You might notice that someone's on their own, a little to the outside of the group. I was often isolated when I was young so I notice people in the same position. One of the ways that is easiest for me to connect when walking into a room is to find people on their own who might be having trouble connecting. If you are already in a group you can introduce people who are on their own into that group. "Ah! Have you met this person and that person?"

I experienced this kind of welcome recently at Brendon Burchard's Expert Academy where people were in groups of five, each sharing their stories for two minutes. I couldn't see a group of four to join, so I stood on the edge of a group of strangers who had started sharing and very quickly one pulled me in saying, "Join us!" Being a little unwell I had less energy to connect so I didn't mind being on the outside, but I was so touched by her welcome. Then after everyone had shared they turned to me, even though the time was up and they could have gone to get coffee.

Becky Cashman's welcome had made me part of the group and they all said "Share your story!" As we took our seats ready for the next session she asked me if I'd have dinner with her that night. We ate downstairs with a few others who Becky had invited and it was really cool to be reminded of how good it is to be welcomed and included.

If you're not ready to jump in, whether you consider yourself an introvert or an extrovert, you can watch what's going on for a moment and see the dynamics. I think some people feel like they always have to be part of a group, whereas with natural curiosity you can sit back now and then and see what's going on. It's very hard to do that if you're desperate to be in the middle of another group. If you keep to yourself for too long though, you can appear distant and uninterested or detached, and people will feel less inclined to include you because they might expect rejection from you.

Be your authentic self. Connecting in this way becomes a key that unlocks possibilities that you may not have imagined. Insincere people merely tolerate others, while genuine connections build trust and ultimately become great relationships.

Rather than wondering if your questions are 'quality enough' remember that there are no silly questions … they might just seem silly to you. Just ASK. This relates to getting to really know people who are already known to you, but not well. Be curious. Know that there's more to that lady you pass in the street, or sit near at church, or see backing out of the driveway next door to you. Everyone has a story, stuff that matters to them, stuff that lights them up. It's okay to say, "I just wanted to say hi. I see you around but we've never had a conversation. How are you?"

It doesn't always go well but it can be turned around. Be curious instead of easily offended, as we might learn something of ourselves and at the same time support that person more than we could realise. If you come over as confident it may highlight in others their own feeling of intimidation and suspicion. What is going on here? What is it that the other person is feeling? Is it uncertainty?

There is a risk of being misunderstood. I had this experience talking to a lady on a jetty along the beautiful Perth coastline. She said, "Have you caught anything?" I replied, "No, I am not fishing but our friend here has just started". She said, "Oh", so I could have stopped there but she had initiated a conversation. So I asked her, "Are you from around here?" I was a little surprised by her tone when she answered "yes" a little defensively or suspiciously. We don't know why people respond like this but sometimes they do. If she had assumed I was a local, she might have thought I was implying she was a foreigner or tourist and therefore unwelcome if that had been her experience before. Or she may have wondered if I wanted to know which beach house was hers, which would be too personal. Feeling the subtle tension I said, "I'm from New South Wales". She replied, "Oh really", and became friendly again.

Later that evening it occurred to me how important it is for people to feel the sense of belonging. My statement may have been similar to one she hears regularly with a darker meaning attached. It may have unearthed an insecurity or prejudice she faces. That is why I responded with where I was from to show I was the 'foreigner'. I was giving her back a sense of status. You could say, it is just one person so does it really matter? Does it bother me if a total stranger is offended? A different question is did I cause offence? So I want to take responsibility and leave her happier, not feeling confused or judged. It comes down to caring for people and fixing a mistake before it causes further harm. People can take it to the extreme and to try to fix the other person's belief system or make amends for years of misunderstanding and judgements. You are only responsible for that moment and that conversation. In saying that you are not fully responsible because they make assumptions too, but if I can leave them in a better, happier place, that's great. If they are in the same place, that is fine also.

Some questions roll off the tongue, but they may not be useful and may be quite damaging. You want a question that results in a better conversation. Of course no two brains are alike, so a question that lands well with one person may not land so well with another because we have completely different neural networks.

For example, the "Are you a local?" question to a local who loves the area and has always lived there may fill them with a sense of pride and they joyfully say yes. To another person the same question with the same tone of voice and expression might have a negative impact if they would like to feel like a local but haven't felt included in the community yet. There could be a whole lot of pain associated with that. It could be like saying "Are you one of the 'in crowd'"? and it is painful to have to say no. This is why it's important to be present with the person you are talking to so you can feel the change, move with it and adapt.

Potentially unhelpful questions:

- "What do you do?"
- "Where are you from?"

Better questions:

- "What do you love to do?"
- "Are you from around here?"

Unhelpful questions may trigger a threat to our social brain and needs. A social threat can cause the same response in the brain as a physical threat. It can distract from the brain thinking clearly and focus the person on escape. The social threats have been well communicated in David Rock's SCARF model (Status, Certainty, Autonomy, Relatedness and Fairness). We can threaten someone's social needs, or they already come with preconceived beliefs and a history of these needs not being met, therefore creating hypersensitive reactions. We need to be aware of our social needs and how they can be threatened or safe and happy.

For our brain to be happy we need a sense of status, certainty, autonomy, relatedness and fairness. The emotional centre of our brain is on high alert, looking for threats in these areas. To look into this further, check out www.neuroleadership.com which I highly recommend.

Status

Where do we rank other people? Do we see people and ourselves as more or less important or clever or significant than others? It's very useful to see others as equals. We have different roles and titles, and varying levels of education and opportunity, but we're all human beings who want to love and be loved, who want to feel connected. Threats to status and feeling 'looked down on' might be caused by:

- comments that diminish someone
- the word JUST – "Do you just work here in the café?" or "Are you just a mum?"
- statements we make about ourselves that make us look important – you might be increasing your own sense of status but diminishing another's, which will cause a disconnect
- being ignored – walk into a café when the staff standing behind

the counter are not taking any interest in you; the longer you wait the more your sense of status decreases because the message you're getting is that they don't think you are important.

Certainty

There is no certainty in life but the brain craves certainty and likes to know what is going to happen. We want to know what time someone will turn up or if someone will do what they said they will do. Our need for certainty can be threatened by thoughts of:

- "Am I in the right place?" "Is this the right venue?"
- "Are they looking at me? Who is that? Should I know that person?"
- "What is expected of me?"

Autonomy

We want to have a choice and a sense of being in control. Threats to autonomy include:

- contradicting choices or imposing views of the world
- someone being bossy
- people jumping queues, even unintentionally.

Relatedness

This is a sense of connection with others around us. We desire that all of our emotional needs be met. Just like physical needs (shelter, food, water, air, safety) we prioritise them individually according to our own wiring. While all of these alerts to the brain are important to consider, I'll spend more time on this area because it is particularly relevant to connecting with others.

Threats to relatedness can include:

- Not smiling – a neutral expression is read by your brain as a threat.
- Not having name-tags – trying to remember someone's name after they've been introduced, and the more you try to remember, or bluff your way through, the harder it is to think straight.
- Looking around the room for someone else while you're 'listening' to someone. I'm sure it's happened to you – someone asks you a question and as you start answering you feel like they're looking for someone 'more important' to enter the room.
- Being overdressed is something to be aware of. Personally I would rather be overdressed than underdressed, but people can be threatened by you 'looking better' than them.

Ways to address these threats – to mininise or eliminate them, or recover from the threat state – include:

- smile and be happy
- be open and curious, without being over the top
- look for something to acknowledge
- be natural – stop trying so hard as people feel it
- give your full attention to the person or people you're with – be IN the conversation
- use people's names:
    1. to remember their name, associate it with something if you can (does it rhyme with something, is it the same name as your mum/dad, cousin or friend?)
    2. repeat it, and clarify how it is spelt or pronounced because the more you think about it, the more you'll remember it, and the more they'll feel that they matter
    3. write it down, see it, and use it – introduce them to someone else if you can.

Fairness

We all know what it is like to feel something that is 'just not fair'. We might hear that statement from children, but it is still important for adults. To establish fairness:

- when pouring yourself a drink, pour an extra one and offer it to someone nearby
- moving your bag off the seat – it is only fair to move it once the train is filling up - and it's a welcoming gesture.
- wait in line when you can, and let someone else in ahead of you, especially if you arrive at the end of the queue almost at the same time.

Pressure or pleasure?

Are you creating a sense of 'pressure' or 'pleasure'? ☹☺

These threats to the brain add pressure and you can't think clearly when you're under pressure. I'm sure you've had plenty of moments of trying to remember someone's name as they walk towards you. You might say hello, but once they've gone and you've given up, their name comes to you. These potential pressures, when you're aware of them, can be turned into an opportunity for pleasure. You can give people a sense of pleasure when you use their name, when you look at them and give them your full attention.

"Remember that a man's name is to him the sweetest and most important sound in any language" – Dale Carnegie

COACHING CORNER

Think about how you can be your best self:

- Start by listing your qualities. (It might be a challenge to do this, and if it is I especially recommend it.)
- What have you been acknowledged for in the past? There will be some common themes.
- What would you like to be acknowledged for? If you would like to be acknowledged for being warm and friendly it's in you already or it wouldn't have come to mind. It may be buried under a sense of inadequacy.

Remember, we don't know what someone else has faced just before they walk into the room. Just as sometimes you've had other things on your mind that have nothing to do with the next event, others you meet could be dealing with any kind of crisis. If you're preoccupied, you may feel a bit nervous or uncomfortable about joining in on the conversation so what's needed is a fresh perspective. Reframe the situation – see it differently.

Consider how you feel as you enter a room full of people. Is it comfortable and exciting? What about when you turn up to a friend's party? Then think of another situation where you went to a function and felt uncomfortable or terrified. To look at the situation from a different angle you might choose to notice how nervousness feels similar to excitement – and decide that you're excited rather than nervous.

With a feeling of uncertainty, we could reframe that and see it in a more positive way. Instead of seeing uncertainty as a negative thing, it could be seeing it as a new learning experience or potential inspiration. Feeling nervous and feeling excited are very similar emotions, so we can just switch those around. It's about being aware of it. So if you notice feeling a bit nervous, a bit anticipatory, then choose what you want to think. Those thoughts might be, "Okay, this is a bit unusual for me". This is different. I wonder what I'll learn today. Or choosing to say, "I will look for the spirit of adventure". It's about just having a visual or having some words that change it from discomfort to something that you are comfortable with. If you like learning say, "Hmm, I might learn something interesting here".

It's a 'growth mindset' as described by Professor Carol Dweck to choose curiosity. We can take things at face value and if it looks uncomfortable we can avoid it (a 'fixed mindset') or we can step forward with curiosity and think what can I learn here or what I can contribute. To choose to reframe something is about being curious and asking yourself, how else could I see this?

There is a great reframe example in the Lego movie song "Everything is awesome" in the line, "Lost my job, it's a new opportunity – more free time for my awesome community".

I recently ran a survey about how people feel when talking to strangers. The good news is that if you feel uncomfortable and nervous about speaking to one or many, you're not alone. Some people are more nervous with public speaking. They're happy to have a chat with people on the bus. They'll chat with a checkout person. They'll talk to anyone. They're good talking to small groups. But put them in front of a crowd, put a microphone in their hand, and it's like, whoa! That's terrifying.

Then there are others who are happy to do the public speaking and actually love it, but the one-on-one or small group situations are terrifying. The desire to be more confident about public speaking is similar to wanting to be more confident on a one-on-one basis because the nerves or confidence starts with the conversation in your head.

The best little piece of information I could share is that if you're nervous, it's because you're thinking about yourself, not your audience.

When we think about it, especially in the context of public speaking, someone says, "Let's welcome to the stage... (insert your name here)", then everyone starts clapping. The attention is on YOU so it's natural to feel some butterflies. If you shift that focus, perhaps towards your audience and what you're there for, the butterflies will settle. I saw this done beautifully by a high school student in Cambodia recently. She introduced herself as Thoeu and started by thanking everyone for coming and thanking us for supporting their scholarships. Her intention in speaking was to express her gratitude and she spoke from the heart. It was incredible. I thought 'that's the essence of great public speaking' and told her that afterwards as she hugged me with gratitude and joy (leaving a big imprint in my heart).

When you're walking into a room or dialing into a teleconference, ask yourself what your intention is in being there.

- Do you want to express gratitude?
- Do you want to bring a sense of curiosity?
- Do you want to come and learn something?

Our mind is often on autopilot, and unless we start noticing what the internal conversation is, we'll be reacting from nerves and discomfort and not connecting as effectively and authentically as we could.

One of the ways that I think we can start shifting our thinking is by reflecting on moments that we have done well, the times when we have been completely present and in the zone. We are very good at analysing and dwelling on the times when we didn't do so well. Don't beat yourself up, but be curious. Reflect on the moments where you have been completely present with an attitude of curiosity or a focus on others.

Have you ever connected with someone who might know you better than you know them? Perhaps you're in the papers or have an online presence. You may not remember or know their name. It's better to be honest and say "I'm sorry. I can't think of your name…" or "I'm not sure if we've met before". Sometimes, I think I have met someone and they say, "Oh, I don't think so". I say, "No worries – well we're meeting now!" I found that honesty helps, because otherwise we get more and more intense on the inside and put up all these inauthentic walls.

If you're public speaking, meeting someone or going for a job interview, you may be wondering "What is expected of me right now?" That puts so much pressure on you but refocusing helps. Choose to be present, honest, and willing to ask questions.

The pressure to remember someone's name, to look professional and other expectations you might have of yourself actually decreases not only your ability to be relaxed and present, but also robs you of creativity. This affects problem solving and memory recall, so it's even harder to solve the 'what is their name?' dilemma.

If you're feeling nervous about connecting with people, you can always say, "This might be a bit awkward" or "I'm a bit nervous to ask you this, but can I ask … ?" Generally, when we confess something like that, people are most likely going to respond by saying, "That's okay". They then connect even more – because you've been vulnerable. Vulnerability is an amazing connector. As Dr Brené Brown, author of *Daring Greatly* says, "Vulnerability is the birthplace of all the positives like belonging, courage, love, creativity and innovation. Vulnerability opens doors of possibility and opportunity".

We interact with strangers all the time and often don't think about it. Consider your connections recently that went well and ask yourself how was your thinking in that moment? What was the quality of your thinking? I know that when I ask this kind of question, people immediately think of moments that didn't go well rather than what did. That's okay. Let it go. So what can you learn from your pleasant interactions? What works? It's probably tiny things.

Then think of an occasion in the last week where you connected with someone and it was just clunky. Notice what you were thinking at the time and then, in hindsight, how you would have changed that clunky interaction for the better. See the opportunities to be curious, compassionate or adventurous.

COACHING CORNER

List:

WINS   CHALLENGES

Moving on:

- Would being more curious help, and what would this look like?*
- Would being more compassionate help, and what would this look like?*
- Would being more adventurous help, and what would this look like?*

For example – Asking quality questions, noticing things to acknowledge, googling/preparing

It's important to note the tone of conversation, whether it's based in positivity or negativity. Notice – does it lift you up or take you down? Does it flatten you, even slightly? If it is based in negativity, which is often what you hear people start a conversation with, it won't go very far, and it won't go so well either. Here's an example – "Shocking weather isn't it?"

When the focus is negative it just takes you down and you start feeling more and more unpleasant. It only changes if you become aware and decide to change direction. This is when you begin to take charge of what goes in and out of your head.

When I was 19, a close friend I lived with at the time told me that I was the most negative person she knew! She explained that she no longer asked me how my day was as my response was usually a complaint. I was shocked. I never wanted to walk negativity into anyone's day, but I had been doing it unaware, processing my problems verbally, and not focusing on the best aspects of the day or being grateful for anything. The brain naturally tends toward a negative focus, and its ability to identify threats is a gift, but one to be aware of and used wisely.

Whichever way you're heading is the way that you'll continue to go unless you change course. Millions of little things can cause a shift. Walking out into the sun can move you further into a positive frame of mind, unless you have a headache – so you might choose chocolate, sleep, sunglasses or whatever works for you. Asking someone about the 'best place' they ever visited, or the most inspiring leader they know of, can shift a conversation from the 'worst place/person/thing' to something that makes them (and you) smile.

And it's best to be honest – don't try to manipulate the conversation. But if you need a segue, just say what you feel – for example, "I lose energy when I talk about politics, can we talk about something that makes us smile instead?" or "I'd love to ask you who or what inspired you to travel …"

We ask better questions when we're in a more positive frame of mind. There's more on this in the chapter called Right Attitude, so for now, just consider what questions you might ask someone when you're happy, curious and carefree.

Perhaps you could go for a walk with someone and ask them to share what they notice. It's always useful to hear another perspective and see things with fresh eyes. One day I was walking with Lyndon and said 'oh, that's beautiful'. He thought we were seeing the same thing. I was looking at the house on the hill in the distance, while he was looking at two trees nearby. Those trees were actually exactly on either side of the house in the distance, creating a frame for my beautiful picture. Our view was then enriched by our shared perspectives.

Our views in life are enriched when we listen to each other.

Consider - *What is your favourite topic of conversation? For example, a hobby, interest or sport. Find where others with a shared interest might connect, and introduce yourself.*

Interest in others

Listen to others with genuine interest in what they're saying. You might need to CHOOSE to be interested. If you want people to be interested in you, express interest in them, and those who matter to them. As St Francis of Assisi expressed so beautifully, "Grant that I may not so much seek to be understood, as to understand…" It's a choice to focus on others first, to understand and value another, when we want to be understood and valued. It's a generous mindset and a humble one.

The heart and science of connecting

A key component of connecting is the heart of listening for potential. My past 10 years of coaching, which is described as an art and a science, has taught me so much about listening and connecting powerfully to serve another person's thinking.

Connecting with someone without agenda or attachment is more about the heart, so I call this the heart and science of connecting. Whether it's with the person in the deli, or the guy at the checkout, your attitude towards them is very much coming from the heart. It's not just a science, and it's not just an art that you might practice for connecting with strangers in a room of people you're doing a sales presentation for. A little deeper is the heart and science of listening and listening for potential, for possibility, for ideas, and for connection. If your heart has a negative attitude towards people of a particular nationality, for example, it will come out of your mouth – sometimes when you least want it to.

"Out of the heart the mouth speaks" - Proverbs 4:23

Interested enough to LISTEN

Maybe today you'll have a conversation with someone. Can I ask you to take note of what you're listening for because we can listen for an opportunity to say something, especially if there's a group of three or four people around and you think, "Ooh! I've got a story about that". So we're listening for the opportunity to jump in and tell that story. We can listen for the question that they're asking so that we can answer that, perhaps to look smart. Or you can listen for what they are really saying, without judgement, and without jumping ahead. Are you open for them to say something new? If your attitude is 'I've heard it all before' you won't listen in the same way as a lifelong learner.

When you're talking, the person who is listening has a lot of things going on in their brain. Even while I'm hearing what you're saying and wanting to be completely present, I'm also thinking, "Yes, yes! I get that". It's about the quality of listening. How long since you've really felt listened to? Perhaps it was a complete stranger on a train or in a hospital waiting room who really heard you and just let you talk.

Practice - *Show interest in others. Begin by listening to a child. Ask a question about something that's important to them, tuning intently into what they're saying. They won't know you're practicing; they'll feel very special, and you'll learn how to pay attention and immerse yourself in someone else's story.*

For my birthday in 2013, I challenged myself to a 'silent day'. I was silent the whole day – in listen-only mode. The idea had come to me as I was swimming laps (where I often get crazy ideas and amazing insights) and I was pondering the importance of listening and what a gift it is that we can give another. I was also thinking of the children of Papua New Guinea (PNG) and their lack of health care and education, considering how I could raise money for the work of Kokoda Track Foundation. Then in the background was the unrelated question, "What am I going to do for my birthday?" These varied subjects all came together in one idea – put the spotlight on listening, and on education needs in PNG, and celebrate my birthday at the same time!

During my silent day I sat myself in a café and invited people to come and have a coaching session where they would do all the talking and thinking. To get them started or encourage their flow of thoughts I wrote the occasional comment or question. Those who booked a time with me had the opportunity to talk as much as they liked and I fully listened. When they were stuck, I wrote things that supported their thinking rather than taking it in a different direction. My feedback included comments like, "How important is this to you?" or "What's the impact of thinking through that?" and "Well done". The insights that they had were extraordinary because their thinking wasn't interrupted or taken off course. The only questions that I asked (silently) helped them to continue to unpack what they were thinking.

One guy came who naturally lets others do most of the talking. He would ask for my advice and want my opinion. I encouraged him to talk through what was on his mind, which was a business challenge. He said,

"Wow, I can't believe I said all that. I really needed to get that off my chest, and I feel so much clearer now. I know how to move forward from here". Listening to people is an extraordinary gift and one that the more we develop, the more we make a difference in the world, and the more people will trust you and want to come back and talk to you.

John Maxwell says, "People don't care how much you know until they know how much you care". Listening to people is a most amazing way of letting people know that you care. It will open the door to more conversations. I would say it helps you to actually be of service in your day-to-day life no matter what we're doing. It's in that action of listening where you can be of service. You don't even necessarily realise it, but expressing gratitude and appreciation is giving people that moment of acknowledging their service no matter what it is.

Mindfulness

People might think that mindfulness is a meditative religious thing but it is a science and it's gaining momentum in the corporate world as it actually makes a significant difference. I first heard about mindfulness in the leadership world when Dr Craig Hassed spoke at the 2008 Neuroleadership Summit, making the science of managing stress easy to understand and practical. Neuroscientists see mindfulness as an essential part of healthy thinking, essential for leadership, for effectiveness in 'getting stuff done'.

Next time you are listening to someone, are you aware of the conversation in your head? Are you completely hearing what they are saying with nothing else going on or do you notice that you're trying to think of the right question to ask? Or the story you want to tell that they have just reminded you of? Sometimes you will notice that your story is better than theirs (in your head). We might be sharing because we think they will be interested or we are trying to regain the limelight. It is important to observe our thinking – not to judge it – but to let it go. Other people notice when you are present because it is actually rare. In general people don't know what it is like to be really listened too. People notice when others are distracted because it is the norm, it's autopilot. When you are on autopilot and living a fast-paced life, it is hard to notice what is going on around you.

Natural confidence (you have more than you think)

You have natural confidence – even if you think you don't. Let me share an example.

In discussing this aspect of the ASKING model, a friend immediately said "but I don't have 'natural confidence' to talk to people" and I replied "Yes you do. I saw you on the weekend, talking to someone who would probably say the same of himself – but you were talking quite enthusiastically together. I saw your natural confidence." The reason these 'introvert' friends of mine connected so confidently was that they discovered that they're both interested in a particular culture and language. If you are talking about something you know and love, you'll communicate far more confidently than a topic that bores or challenges you.

Confidence is one of those things that comes and goes at different stages throughout life. Some people say they were more confident when they were young. Someone older might say they have gained confidence as they aged. It depends on so many different factors that are going on in our world. We all suffer blows to our confidence, perhaps due to everyday things not going well, a job loss, or a series of disappointments. If we start blaming ourselves or taking on board what people have said our confidence can take a dive. We can make sense of the positive or negative thoughts in our head and we'll believe whatever we're most focused on.

Comparing ourselves to other people or to picture-perfect images in the media makes us lose confidence. Have you ever compared yourself to someone who looks fabulous or speaks with eloquence? What you are seeing and hearing is their external world. It is like you are seeing them on stage. In contrast what you know of your world is all of the back stage activity, the chaotic, messy images and words everywhere, and it is not what you actually express. It's not what the world sees.

That eloquent person you are comparing yourself to has their behind the scenes activity going on too. You don't see or hear that. When you speak you hear all the rush of words you could say, as you think so much faster than you speak, and your audience (of one or many) only hears the words that come out. This is the back stage chaos going behind the scenes as the centre stage performance takes place.

In a meeting with a large organisation I was having a conversation with four managers, but one of them was looking at me very seriously. I thought that this was a great example of an opportunity to misread someone's thoughtfulness. I didn't know whether I was connecting with him. I wondered to myself, is he not impressed, or is he just focused? I noticed that my thinking could keep me from completely connecting with the whole group. So I decided that he was really focused and curious. Then I could let go of the concern and be fully present in the group and more able to serve each of them.

When you relate to someone, saying to yourself, "I know exactly what you mean", you are relating to your own stories. You can make the choice to listen – the choice that this moment is about someone else. One thing that we can do that transforms conversations is let it be about the person who is talking, noticing and thinking. Say to yourself, it's fine that I am here listening to this story right now. Leadership coaches do this, which accelerates people's growth. You can do this too. Be totally with the person and make the decision to stay with them.

Our brain does go to other places. It is natural that our brains make connections so we don't need to be beat ourselves up about that. The key thing is how quickly we catch ourselves and come back to the present moment. It just takes practice. It is also about noticing, and reflecting on the 'well done' moments, rather than focusing on the moments where you missed the mark and your attention wandered off.

It is useful to look at the science of great questions or the heart and science of listening for potential. They are both relevant because sometimes we ask ourselves the question, "How do they want me to respond?" We could just ask them, "How can I best help you here?" Sometimes people don't actually know what they want when they ask for your advice. In fact they don't really want advice – they just want a listening ear.

Building and rebuilding confidence is important. There might be specific moments that you recall, thinking, "Oh yeah, that was when I lost confidence". One of the many times in my life when my confidence took a significant hit was when I was in hospital with my newborn son. He was born with a cleft lip which contributed a rough start and while some of the nurses were clearly born for their role, others tore at my confidence with their criticisms, arrogance and generally negative attitude.

Another confidence deflator is not only comparing yourself to others, but to the 'dream you', the future you that you have not become yet. It comes back to an expectation of "I should have been more… by now". I am sure that I am not alone in putting those kinds of expectations on myself. It drains our confidence to compare or put pressure on ourselves.

When we go to a function and we see everyone dressed beautifully we don't realise that these beautiful people may have gone through three pairs of stockings that morning. They might have been yelling at the kids just before they turned off their temper to step into the public eye and look so calm and beautiful. So it is not fair comparing ourselves with others. This is the difference between backstage chaos and centre stage finesse.

What else do you think erodes your confidence? If you hear someone being critical of other people you may start thinking, "What do they say about me?" You could take those thoughts in a worrying cycle downwards, so it is good to notice that thinking and put a stop to it.

What often stops us connecting well with others is what our brain is doing at the time. If you start worrying as you drive away from home that you didn't turn the iron off, your confidence decreases. You may worry to the point where you've lost confidence that you turned the iron off and have to turn around and go back home.

You might be worrying about the state of your office and in doing so lose confidence in other areas like connecting with people. Our confidence grows when we do something brave. It could be speaking in front of 10 people or doing a physical challenge such as a high ropes course. When we do something for the first time, our confidence grows.

I think this question is a great one to ask yourself regularly – when was the last time that you did something for the first time?

Our confidence grows when:

- We do something brave.
- We do something for the first time.
- We do something well, we realise it and/or get recognition.

Our confidence doesn't necessarily grow when we do something well. How many times do we not give ourselves credit for something that we have done well? When you do things that are normal for you, you probably do them easily and effortlessly. It comes so naturally that you don't recognise the skill involved. It may not be until someone notices your work that you realise you have achieved something. You do things on autopilot and you don't necessarily realise the steps that it has taken to get to that place of competence.

It is time for us to be more aware of our strengths, and allow ourselves to accept praise. Sometimes it takes external recognition to actually consider, "That wasn't too bad was it?". Accepting praise and acknowledging your talents or work is a great way to build confidence and learn more about yourself.

I want people to feel valued. I realise that I might be the only person who smiled at them that day. I want to brighten someone's day. It matters because people matter.

When talking to a stranger you might offer a compliment, which could build your confidence as well as theirs. When you give something that is well received it's a boost to both giver and receiver. On the other hand, if you're given a compliment, don't overthink it or judge it, simply accept it. How many times, have we pushed aside a compliment or acknowledgement and missed the opportunity for insight? Build the discipline to look at the positive rather than the negative, not looking at what you didn't do so well but rather focusing on what you did do well.

Another thing that will diminish your confidence is a lack of clarity – whether it's about your goals or your knowledge of a topic. So whenever possible, speak about things you know and love. Your passion and enthusiasm will make it easy for people to connect with you.

COACHING CORNER

Let's spend some time thinking about connecting confidently.

• What matters most to you about connecting with others? For example, sharing your passion, learning new things, making someone's day, finding like-minded people...

Gratitude

After the amazing experience you have just had by following the first five steps of ASKING, we are left with one of the most important aspects of talking to strangers and connecting with others. In fact it is one of life's best lessons – gratitude.

Gratitude is the quality of being thankful. It is readiness to show appreciation and to return kindness. Gratitude unlocks more confidence, learning and connectedness. When we reflect on our conversations, we could beat ourselves up about how we could have done better, the opportunity we missed or what we 'should have' or 'could have' said or done differently, or we could be grateful for the connection. The first option is our most common response, but when we're grateful – everything changes. Consider being grateful for:

- The times when someone has smiled/connected with us.
- The times we've made a new friend.
- The times a stranger has put a smile on your face, perhaps in a moment of passing by with a child or a pet.
- The moments of customer service that have left you feeling satisfied, delighted or excited. Think about the transactions where you felt happier than you expected to. That feeling probably resulted more from the interaction than the actual spend. Like my speeding fine delivered by a gracious, friendly and forgiving policeman. (He could have fined me a greater amount, but gave me the lowest fine. I was very grateful!)

Gratitude is an attitude that can be developed, a habit that is incredibly satisfying and rewarding.

Tips to increase your attitude of gratitude:

- Look for opportunities to say, "Thank you" or "I'm grateful for…" or "I appreciate…".
- Be mindful and sincere. A quick "Thanks mate" is not as sincere or memorable as "Thank you – I appreciate your …".
- Be specific, such as "I appreciate your comments" or "your ideas".
- Write it down! Challenge yourself to write three things you're

grateful for when you wake up and when you go to bed. Perhaps when you stop for a lunch break or go for a walk. This is a great perspective shifter. Even if you don't FEEL grateful, choose to be and write. "I am grateful to be alive", "I am grateful that I have ..." – even the simple things like air to breathe, blood moving through your body, the ability to move.

- Write it down and send it! Sharing your gratitude with someone else will make your day as well as theirs. Have you been inspired by someone? Send them a note. It can cause a massive ripple effect.

Reflecting on the ASKING model

I'm sure you're already noticing these elements in your everyday conversation. You'll also notice that they don't have to be in the A-G order of ASKING. In the next part of this book, I'll share stories that demonstrate how these elements can be applied.

PART TWO

How to **connect**
with anyone, anywhere

CONNECT AND ENCOUNTER

Infinite possibilities for connection exist, and the following examples cover a wide range of scenarios that will remind you of your own connections and inspire you to see more possibilities. You'll find yourself becoming more open, responsive and proactive in connecting and you'll be more aware of choosing your attitude and approach. You'll see extraordinary doors of opportunity opening up for yourself and many others.

We'll begin with Customer Service as we have so many encounters in this environment, then explore more opportunities for connection, literally with anyone, anywhere.

Customer service

In this chapter we will address delivering customer service to strangers and interacting with others as a customer ourselves. You may not have drawn the connection between customers and strangers, but every customer was a stranger at some time. I've found that a genuine connection leads to more sales, and happy customers don't ask for refunds. In several sales roles I've held, from furniture and clothing to coach training, I've gained valuable insights and seen that it's more about human connection than complicated sales processes. In my retail experience many years ago I broke sales records in two different companies and at the time it was a mystery to me how this was happening.

As the provider of customer service

The secret to great customer service is that you're not serving people who are paying money, you're serving people. If you value people above profit you will connect authentically and serve with joy whether you're serving or being served, paying or being paid. It's about welcoming people, being an ambassador for your product, service, town or community. It's about being generous with your time and energy, valuing people because they are fellow human beings. It's about being aware of small ways in which you can make the world a brighter place.

Customer service is an opportunity to make someone's day! To give them hope and a little encouragement! It's easy to be so focused on the tasks at hand that the importance of people can be forgotten. The problem with customer service is in our heads – and the solution is in our heads too. We just need to raise awareness, reflect on what works, and create opportunities to contribute to others.

My greatest lesson about customer service developed in the most unlikely place – working in a dental surgery 20 years ago. People do not want to be there and they bring their fears and anxiety with them. I became so aware of how people felt and that it is so important to acknowledge and address their emotional needs, not just the most obvious practical needs. Even in a dental surgery you can provide an experience that people are so delighted, relieved, comfortable and surprised about that they want to come back – and will refer you to as many people as they possibly can!

Even in an unpopular, but essential industry, you have the opportunity to be creative and surprise people by going above and beyond what's expected. It's in your enthusiastic, warm greeting, your beautiful stationery, the painting on the ceiling, the cup of tea while you wait, the explanation of the work to be done, a touch on the shoulder or a hand to hold. We didn't have the extras that we see in modern practices now, however, there were plenty of hand-holding moments when someone was so nervous about a needle or extraction.

I remember one lady holding my hand so tight I wondered how her long fake nails didn't cut my hand, but her anxiety was so great I was pleased to be there for her.

The greatest challenges in customer situations of any kind are usually the basic challenges of human interaction. We all see the world differently! Every single brain is different. No-one else will think about things quite like you do, but our basic needs are the same. Consider how you want to be treated. Can you provide that experience for others? How would you want your mother or grandmother to be treated? What do you notice about your best moments, not just as a customer, but also in any business interaction? What do we do when we have an exceptional experience? We tell people about it and we go back and spend more. We love doing business with people who make us feel like the sun is shining that little bit brighter and warmer – or refresh us like a cool breeze on a hot day!

A local café served me a cappuccino with the word "Enjoy" written across it in chocolate sauce. I was so delighted I took a photo and shared it across social media, which caused great excitement. If it's really great or really poor, that's when it's talked about it. There are so many opportunities to take poor or average situations and give people a positive experience they'll 'shout it from the rooftops'. I've had a disappointing experience in a local restaurant, but when I discussed it with the manager he not only resolved the issue but went further by giving us a round of drinks. His apologetic and receptive manner and his clear dedication to customer delight completely turned the situation around and we've recommended them and returned there since.

FIVE STEPS TO STUNNING CUSTOMER SERVICE

It's about focus. Focus outwardly, on how you can be of service, rather than inwardly. All of that mental chatter about how you look and what others think can really get in the way. Being aware of what you're feeling and thinking, and then being able to change that is powerful. Reappraising and reframing is one of the ways that we can do that, by choosing to see things in a better light.

Step 1: Choose your focus

Come up with a way of thinking about it that is unique and relevant to you. Decide on a focus for the day, the week or the month (it's good to change it every now and then to keep it fresh and fun). It could be something like:

- "I treat my clients with the kindness and respect I'd give my grandmother".
- "I intend to put a smile on everyone's face!"
- "I will give people a spring in their step".
- "I create customer loyalty and raving fans!"
- "I solve people's problems!"

When you design the focus you want to take into your day, use your own words and consider what inspires YOU. When you find a way of energising yourself, you can easily energise others. Be bold and confident, which is easiest when you're being YOU!

COACHING CORNER

- What have I done that has made people smile?
- What has generated more sales than usual or more repeat customers?
- Who do I know with great attention to service?

Step 2: Create Systems

Create systems that support your attention on your chosen focus. It could be prompts like a smiley face or script, near your phone or counter, or hidden in your wallet to be aware of or memorise. That will trigger action that connects you to others with energy, a smile and friendly approach. (It could also be remembering to eat lunch and keep well hydrated!) A smiley face is proven to increase feel-good chemicals such as dopamine in the brain, so this simple icon is not to be overlooked! ☺

COACHING CORNER

- Do I consciously manage my physical and emotional state to be at my best?
- What systems and habits can I create to support my focus on others?

Step 3: Create opportunities

It's time to brainstorm and put all your ideas on paper. Perhaps you can ask for support. Who do you know that is passionate about customer service? When you start focusing on all the possible options, you'll be amazed at the ideas that come to you.

List all the free possibilities, and all the low-cost ones, and focus on these first. A smile is free, a bowl of lollies is very inexpensive, and a colourful stamp or sticker for visiting children can make the spender's experience far more pleasant for them and more lucrative for you.

COACHING CORNER

- What steps can I take, now that I see more ideas and opportunities?
- What will I do first and what can I create a system for?
- How will I continue to be aware of my own thinking and what goes on around me?

Step 4: Be the customer you want to serve

I was in a remote town, which apparently is known for bad customer service. I commented to my friend as I walked out of a store that all I've seen is great customer service. To which she replied, "But Kerrie, you created that positive experience. You spoke cheerfully to the girl at the checkout, she looked up to find you smiling at her, taking an interest in her – of course she'll be nice to you".

Unfortunately, many customers expect great customer service, but don't turn up as a 'great customer'. Make it easy for yourself and for those who serve you! I love being a great customer at every opportunity, from when I shop or dine out, to attending appointments. When someone delivers a cup of coffee to my table, I look them in the eye and thank them. If I have an opportunity, I will acknowledge them for something they've done well, for example, being prompt or looking fabulous. I believe that as we focus on the good, we see more of it.

Raise your own awareness of what you focus on. If you've ever ridden a bike, you'll know that if you see the holes in the road and focus on that, saying "I'm not going to hit it, I'm not going to hit it", you know you'll hit it for sure! Focus on the best part of the road, and up ahead, that's where you will end up.

One of the most important things for me is to make people feel important. When shopping I make it a point to thank staff for what they're doing and tell them they've done a great job. My intention is to help them to feel important and valued. We don't always acknowledge being served or interact when we're serving people.

Going through the checkout is something we can do without noticing the people around us. It's really lovely when someone appreciates the work you do. You'll never know when that person might pop up in your sphere of influence or business. You never know when and where you might meet this person again. And you never know how much your kindness meant to them. Look people in the eye whenever you can and smile.

COACHING CORNER

- Think about the moments you've experienced that made you smile and feel good; that left you happy to spend money. Go to your favourite business and experience it again – reflecting on these points:

    ✓ What were the small elements that worked well?
    ✓ Did you feel more important or more connected?
    ✓ Were you given the space to make up your own mind?
    ✓ Was it the creativity or unique approach you appreciated?
    ✓ What would make me really want to go back and spend more?
    ✓ What are the little things I appreciate as a customer?

Step 5: Value yourself and others

People are important. You are important. Your thoughts and feelings are important. The essence of my passion for customer service is simply my passion for people. People are important – they are so valuable. We don't have that conversation often enough. We shouldn't place value on people only when we realise they most need it or when we need them. Any opportunity to place value on people, to make them feel special, is not to be missed.

COACHING CORNER

- What opportunities do you see in your day-to-day life to place value on people?
- How can we endeavour to give our best to make someone's life a little brighter?

As the customer

Have you ever walked out of a place of business feeling so much better than you went in, just because of the way someone treated you? At other times, have you left feeling worse than when you arrived, perhaps because of a word, a tone or because you were ignored? I experienced the best and worst examples of customer service in one day recently, and because they were within hours of each other, highlighted to me how easy it is to excel or completely fail in this area.

I can be deliriously happy when I've been served well or when I've observed someone else being the recipient of great service. Whenever I can I celebrate it taking a few moments to acknowledge what has been done well. This results in the 'great service giver' standing taller, seeing that their contribution has made a difference so they continue and even improve their service. Ken Blanchard has made famous the concept of 'catching people doing something right' and acknowledging it. As an extension to that quote – "If you want to grow something – pay attention to it!"

During economic downturns, people are becoming concerned about how their business will withstand the challenges. I truly believe that increasing the level of happiness in a business, bringing fun and creativity to the surface, with a focus on each customer who walks through the door, will stand a business in good stead through any economic fluctuation. Consider this: if the world around you is not positive, where will you want to go? The stores where people put a smile on your face or the ones just going through the motions?

Happiness is absolutely a choice, one that we must make and continue to make if our businesses are going to flourish. Yes, I'm talking about flourishing businesses, because we all know that it's possible. Just as some plants flourish in harsh conditions that would cause others to wilt, some businesses are going to thrive and wonder what all the fuss is about. You can choose to thrive.

These little exchanges are so simple yet so undervalued. The businesses that flourish in 'difficult times' are those that are not focused on how hard things are, but on how easy it is to build a connection with a customer and do the little things that make the biggest difference. It's just a choice to care for people and provide effective and creative customer service.

Customer service is a hot topic and you only need to bring it up in conversation to discover that everyone has an opinion. Did you realise that your opinion says a lot about you? And did you realise that your opinion is your reality; it's your self-fulfilling prophecy? If you think the customer service stinks in your town, that's true for you, but not the truth as a whole. As I mentioned before, bike riders of the world will know – you will hit a ditch if that's what you're focused on. You will find bad customer service is there for the taking. Raise your own awareness of what you're paying attention to. You get what you focus on. So choose your focus.

Are you proud of your neighbourhood, your town or region? I really believe you can be very proud of your community if you seek out the good news stories. They're everywhere!

Where have you experienced the best customer service? What was great about it? Was it one thing or a number of small elements that added up to a great experience? Did you tell them?

I love walking past florists and cafés (going in is nice too) because of the wafting fragrance of flowers and freshly brewing coffee. I feel my day is enriched. How is it that walking past the butcher is also a lift in my day? I'm always greeted with a smile. Always! And I rarely buy meat, being blessed by farming parents. Butchers always have smiling faces and cheery hello's and I'm sure it's the reason for at least half their sales.

It occurs to me that perhaps Bad Customer Service is what's reserved for Bad Customers, and Good Customer Service is how Good Customers are served. Just a thought, and it's not 100% accurate, but it's worth asking yourself – am I a good customer? Do I make it easy for people to serve me? Am I a joy to serve or a hard taskmaster? How could I contribute to the interaction more positively? How quickly could you list your five best customer service experiences? How long would it take to list the worst five?

Unfortunately, the human brain tends toward the negative, so it's all too often that a conversation focuses on what's wrong with something or someone. This is not at all helpful. It doesn't help anyone and it doesn't improve the mood of your day (unless you enjoy the sense of winning the 'most dramatic story' award).

What if you were to ask yourself this question – "What was the best customer service experience I've had lately?"

COACHING CORNER

- How can I deliver better service, or connect positively with people?
- How can I make someone's day a little brighter?

I believe in people. I believe that when I encounter people in their workplace, I'm generally seeing a person who wants to be happy, wants to do well in their work, and wants to make a difference. Sometimes they get tired and wonder if they're getting anywhere, so of course their desire to do good is not so evident. Their best will come out when we give them an opportunity to shine.

FRIENDS IN NEW PLACES

I was a total stranger to a man I drove to Sydney recently after he spoke at a community event in Narromine in New South Wales, a half hour drive from my home and six hours from Sydney. I knew who Sam Cawthorn was because we had mutual friends (on Facebook), several of whom are also well-respected motivational speakers. I heard him speak that night at Narromine and share his story but he only knew me as a 'great audience member' in the front row who smiled and listened attentively.

Sam had flown out to Dubbo, but had to hire a car to get back overnight due to a mix-up with dates. He couldn't get another flight in time for his interstate event the following morning. He certainly was not expecting me or anyone else to offer to drive him to Sydney so it did take a couple of people to convince him that it was best to not tackle the long trip on his own through the night after a big day – he was brave to trust me. I've since been asked, what possessed you to do such a thing? So let's unpack what was going on here:

Factor 1: Empathy and service

I love helping people and it wasn't random help – I know that road, I know the length of time it takes and how much longer it feels when you're on your own. I know what it's like when you've been speaking all day then again at night. After a day like that, you're pumped, you feel like all is well with the world, you feel you could do anything and you forget how exhaustion can hit when it's all over. I also felt empathy for the organisers, who were concerned about Sam driving so far alone and they weren't able to drive him back.

Factor 2: Conversation

I knew we'd connect and have a great conversation. The key reason we spend time with people is that we like them! I had heard Sam speak for an hour and was inspired by his attitude. I am so appreciative of time with people who have a similar attitude to me, and especially if they think bigger than me, people who embrace life like I do and live purposefully. I know my resilience and positivity grows as I spend time with people who are positive and resilient.

Our brains want fairness so we will assess the '"What's in it for me" factor. I knew that I'd enjoy our conversation and take away more learning and inspiration. I was happy to drive him without expectation of him giving anything as I knew he'd been giving of himself all day. But I knew, as I said to him, "We'll have at least an hour of great conversation about our mutual friends, but I'm happy for you to get some sleep".

As a couple of people said as we left the venue, "Mentoring in the car – what a bonus to be spending one-on-one time with a mentor to leaders all over the globe". But I put aside the expectation of this because of Factor 1 - Empathy. I knew he'd had a big day and I let go of this expectation to allow him space to stretch out and sleep so that he could drive later if I needed a break.

I knew that a friendship was possible because of our shared passion for making a positive difference as well as our mutual friends on Facebook. I didn't know at that stage if any of them were close friends or if they were just people who he had met at speaking engagements. I must acknowledge Sam's openness because I was much more of a stranger to him than he was to me. I already had a growing sense of connection because of so many small indicators.

During his presentation he talked about his wife and children. His attitude to his family and his faith spoke volumes, so I knew him to be someone who could easily be a friend. I knew that it would be comfortable in the car and we'd enjoy each other's company, so it would be an enjoyable trip even if a lot of it was spent with one driving and one sleeping. As it turned out, we'd just left town with a good five or more hours ahead of us, and Sam started asking me about my work and especially my dreams and goals. We did talk most of the way – so much for giving him time to sleep!

How did I get to drive the 'celebrity speaker' home five-and-a-half hours and stay in his family home? I met the right people in the right place and I had the right attitude. Sam did too. Right attitude is a choice; right people and place are factors we can partially control by making room in our lives.

RIGHT PEOPLE, RIGHT PLACE, RIGHT ATTITUDE

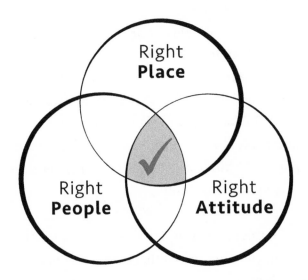

How do we find that sweet spot that connects the right people at the right place with the right attitude? Consider what is right for you as you read my examples. It's very much an 'in the moment thing', an intuitive decision. For me the right place is not just where the action is versus a night at home. I could have stayed home for a quality night in with my husband while my son was at work. (Lyndon actually went out to another function that night, which turned out to be his 'right place' as he connected with someone he was able to encourage.)

I could have spent a night working on this book, as my deadline was getting uncomfortably close. It was not a conscious thought that going out might give me more content – that could be an excuse to go out any day of the week! When you are writing a book, as any author will attest, there are moments when you don't want to sit and write. Being in the right place for me that night was easy because I'd been invited to the event by Helen Jeffery, who was one of the organisers I'd met only a few days earlier. And her guest speaker was someone I knew would have an inspirational story so I wanted to encourage the organisers and help to get more people there. I need inspiring and encouraging too and by me going and promoting it, encouraging others to go, it just helps everyone.

Right place – for me it's where there is life, where I can be encouraged and encourage. I don't go to every event in town or everything I'm invited to. I would be a full-time event attendee if I went to everything. I could easily have said "no thanks" to this event. Two nights earlier I'd been to a fantastic Suncorp Bank event featuring gold medal Olympian, Steven Bradbury. I was already encouraged, inspired and on purpose. But as Zig Ziglar says, "Motivation doesn't last, neither does showering – that's why it's recommended daily".

Right attitude – in this case it was a desire to learn and an attitude of service. When I'm willing to serve others, doors of opportunity open that I didn't even expect.

When Sam was surrounded by people telling him not to drive home alone, and he was saying that he was feeling fine to drive, I wanted to give him autonomy (no-one likes being pushed to make a decision). So I said he didn't even need to decide for half an hour as we would go through Dubbo first and meet at McDonalds for a coffee and then I could leave my car at home. It gave him time to call his wife (I'd already called my husband to run this crazy idea past him), and it gave Sam time to consider the idea.

When we reconnected in McDonalds carpark he asked, "Are you sure? Do you know what you're getting yourself in for?" and I said, "Yes, it's fine! Well actually no – I don't know what I'm in for – it's all part of the adventure. We do this, my Dad does this – we drive people home. It's just that your home is a bit further than someone I'd normally give a lift to. And we talk to strangers and help strangers – actually I'm just about finished writing a book about that". I'm sure you can imagine his response: "Whaaat?!!"

I'm grateful to have connected with Sam and his family, as it has opened doors of opportunity, encouragement and support for so many people beyond the obvious.

COACHING CORNER

- Which elements of the ASKING model did you notice as you read this story?
- Unpack your own recent connection with someone. What supported the conversation to continue? Was it Gratitude? Awareness? What else?

When I first connected with Sam, I was Aware of lots of small things that connected us, such as his music choices, his language around resilience and his inspiring attitude. He was Aware that I was engaged and smiling on the front row. As we walked into McDonalds he commented enthusiastically "Hey you're a great audience member!" Without even realising, I was Starting Small by smiling and listening and taking notes.

I was Aware of the distance and Aware of the organiser's desire to look after their guest. There were lots of small moments of awareness that made it easy to Keep Going with quality questions. Some of these questions were around mutual friends and how we'd connected with them, and these led to deeper questions, in this case Sam asking about my purpose, goals and dreams. I was interested in Sam and his story, which I'd heard some of at the event, and Sam was interested in mine, asking question after question, unpacking insights for both of us. Because Right People, Right Place, Right Attitude was at play, Natural Confidence was there to support a quality connection – which I was very Grateful for!

RIGHT PEOPLE: ANYONE

One of the most delightful things about connecting with strangers that so many people share with me is the unexpected nature of the interaction. It's the fascinating information from the person you least expected it from. Unless we have a conversation, we don't know that the man in shorts and t-shirt you meet on holiday on a sailing boat is tripping around the world with his family for a grandchild's 13th birthday, a trip they do for every grandchild, or that the fellow passenger on a regional flight worked in Buckingham Palace before moving to Australia. These people often appear without airs and graces and if you made the assumption that they're 'just an ordinary person' you could miss the delight and learning from these interactions. There's no such thing as 'just an ordinary person' – everyone is unique and has an interesting and important story.

Famous and influential people

If you want to connect to famous people for the celebrity factor, go and find another book. When I say 'famous and influential people' I am talking about those at the top of their field, not because of their beauty or mere celebrity status or media attention. I mean those who have worked hard to get where they are. The people at the top of their field may be famous and easily obtain media coverage but, most importantly, they are generally people of substance.

I am a people-person and thrive on connecting with others but there are limits on my time, energy and resources. I know that some people get 'peopled out' well before I do and they are happy with their small number of close friends. I appreciate this and don't judge people for leaving an event early. Having a lot of people in your world is not about being famous, unless that's your goal. It's about leadership and influence and caring about people who connect with me.

Mary Kay Ash is a great inspiration. She founded the Mary Kay Cosmetics Company in 1963 and built one of the most significant companies of the 20th century. She was known as an inspiring motivator and visionary entrepreneur and named, among many awards, the 'most influential woman in business during the 20th century'. Her story is worth looking into for her attitude towards people and she built this significant company underpinned by the Golden Rule – "Do to others as you would have them do to you".

She would stay at a function as a long line of women waited to meet and connect with her. She cared about people and would hold their hand and speak with them for a few minutes each, really connecting. They were not long conversations because there was an appreciation that others were waiting, but she would give something to each of them. She was available to connect and it is quite a contrast to a celebrity's wave and smile from a distance before getting whisked away to a limousine. It doesn't have to be a long connection, but if it is authentic people can feel it.

It's only recently that I've seen a brief video of Mary Kay Ash speaking about her decision to connect with people who stood in line to meet her. As a younger woman she had stood in line for three hours to congratulate the vice-president of a company. She said it was a long time for him to be shaking hands with people, as it was a long time for her to wait. When it was finally her turn at the front of the line, so inspired to meet him, he shook her hand without seeing her. He was looking further down the line, probably to see how many more people were there. That was her moment of decision – "If I ever become the person with whom they're shaking hands, I will put my attention on that person".

I've never heard Sir Richard Branson mention Mary Kay, however, he's a great example of being the person who people want to shake hands with, and when I met him in Perth in March 2010, I found him to be just as attentive as Mary Kay was known to be.

Seated at a table, in the midst of 600 business people, I realised that my mission to connect with Sir Richard and give him a copy of my newly published book would not be as easy as I anticipated. However, it was my primary reason for flying East to Sydney, then West across the continent, so I intended to accomplish my goal. I went to see the ushers at the doors near the front of the auditorium and enquired which door Sir Richard would be entering and exiting through and shared with them my desire to give him a copy of my book, *Lifting the Lid on Quiet Achievers*, on behalf of the entrepreneurs featured in it. The ushers told me what time he was due to arrive and where he'd be coming in.

The breakfast commenced with Pat Mesiti speaking first and then Glenn Capelli, whose brilliant presentation made the travel feel completely worthwhile. But I hadn't forgotten my mission. Checking in with the ushers at the appointed time, I was shown the room that led to the back of the stage area. I stood for a few moments with others who must have also been tipped off. When Sir Richard entered the foyer he was preceded by a woman with a commanding presence, marching in, arms wide, declaring, "Everyone needs to clear the room!" Immediately we all stepped back against the walls or out the side doors as he walked through. I thought "Fair enough. He's getting ready to speak. I'll catch up with him afterwards".

I went back into the auditorium to my seat and as Sir Richard took the stage he was not speaking alone, but was on a panel, with previous speakers Pat and Glenn plus several others. It was a very insightful question time, and what I noticed most was the quality of the questions and how Sir Richard responded. Glenn Capelli, who had completely captured my attention with his sense of humour and insightful presentation earlier, seemed to ask the question that best served Sir Richard, a simple, humble question that brought out his vibrancy and passion, which in turn served the audience.

When it was announced that Sir Richard would not be stopping to meet anyone as he had a full schedule, my determination grew. As he left the stage and the host began thanking people and completing the event, I went straight for the foyer to be ready to meet him. As he came out of the auditorium through the door a young man stepped in front of me and asked him to sign a copy of his book, which he did. I waited and then stepped forward holding out my book and said, "Excuse me Sir Richard … I'd like to give you a copy of my book as you are mentioned …". To which he replied, "Oh thank you, that's great".

As he was accepting it and looking at it I continued, "It's regional Australian entrepreneurs stories and we want to thank you for inspiring us. I've tagged these pages (with post-it-notes) where you're quoted or mentioned". He was so delighted, and what I saw and felt most was his genuine appreciation as he gave his full attention to me and to the book in his hands, acknowledging the effort of publishing a book and being an entrepreneur. I was grateful to meet him and see how someone so famous could be so engaged and interested in a stranger when he 'didn't have time' to connect.

An usher handed me back my iPhone after taking a photo of 'the moment' when I'd presented the book, unfortunately capturing me from the neck down. A nice photo of my skirt suit and heels. I'd given another usher my camera, so when I caught a glimpse of the iPhone photo I didn't worry about it. I asked Sir Richard if I could take a photo of him with the usher who'd taken our picture and he was happy to oblige, so I took a lovely photo of her with him as she said, "I don't know if the photo I took of you actually worked". As this was happening his minder was telling him to move, "keep walking, keep walking", as people were coming out of the auditorium. He put his arm around me and said "we'll have to keep walking". I asked if I could take a picture as we walked. I have a 'selfie' of the two of us; a pretty bad photo as the light was behind us but a fun memory of a happy connection.

I went back into the auditorium, grabbed the other copy of the book I'd brought as a spare, and went up the front to see Pat Mesiti, who I'd known since the our involvement in Youth Alive in the 1990s. Pat and I had a quick hello and he said, "I'll be back in a minute". As I stood waiting I saw Glenn Capelli nearby and thanked him for his presentation. We talked for a while and someone took a photo of us holding our books that we'd given each other.

This moment, shared on Facebook, is significant as it is what connected Jane Pelusey and I. The photo of us on Glenn's page caught Jane's eye as she tells in her introduction.

COACHING CORNER

- Which elements of the ASKING model did you notice as you read this story?

When it doesn't go so well

In contrast to my connection with Sir Richard, I remember being in a function room with community leaders awaiting the arrival of then Prime Minister John Howard in February 2000. What would you say to him if you had a chance to meet him? This was the discussion point of the people I was with, people of high standing in the community who I looked up to. I became frustrated that 'talking to the PM' seemed only hypothetical. When the Prime Minister did arrive these people didn't go and talk to him. They left him with his official party and a few local officials. I understand that it's not just the Prime Minister you are approaching, but you're being watched by all of his team as well as the local VIPs who might be judging you and your conversation with the PM.

As we were leaving the venue, I gathered what little confidence I had and stepped forward to ask Mr Howard if I could walk with him. He was happy to walk and talk on the way to his next appointment. I didn't really know what to say but I fumbled through a conversation as we crossed the streets of Dubbo. I rattled off a quote on something meaningful about young people and tried to sound educated. I'm sure I really didn't. I may have chosen a worthy topic, but there was no clear purpose in it. I know it would not have been much different to the many conversations he'd have with countless people but certainly not memorable.

On reflection, it felt like an inauthentic conversation on both sides and I wished I'd just stuck to something non-political. I was just taking the opportunity to talk because I felt no-one else had.

In hindsight, I could have thanked him for his visit to our city and given him my parent's regards. I could have acknowledged the courtesy he showed my mother when she met him in France at a World War

One memorial. My parents and their friends offered him a lift back into town when he realised his transport had gone without him. He insisted mum take the front seat and he climbed in the back of the truck with Dad and a few others. I could have made a personal connection by mentioning that occasion, but I tried to sound educated instead.

Before you can learn anything from an embarrassing situation, you need to let go of the angst you took away from it. No-one else will be tossing and turning over the fact that you could have been more witty or relaxed or conversational. Let it go and look at the situation through curious eyes, not with your critical lenses on. What do you notice? How would you like to communicate? How would this conversation be if you were the person you want to be in that moment?

There is plenty of good news in regional areas

Prime Minister John Howard came very close to telling country people they should count their blessings when he attended an invitation-only lunch at the Amaroo Hotel yesterday.

After a quick bite to eat and a chat with about 80 locals - including members of the clergy, Aboriginal leaders, farmers and business representatives - Mr Howard launched into an upbeat message. Focussing on low

⊔ STREET WALK: Kerrie Phipps representing the Dubbo Ministers Association briefly has the ear of Mr Howard in Macquarie Street.

The Daily Liberal, 2 February, 2000.

I had a purpose in speaking with Sir Richard, while my interaction with Mr Howard was less thought out. If you are going to meet a famous person, have an intention that isn't just about you. I was meeting Sir Richard on behalf of the entrepreneurs in my book. A couple of them would have loved to come with me to the event and we'd quoted and mentioned Sir Richard in our stories.

Now when I meet famous or influential people I speak with them if I have a purpose, not for a photo opportunity. If they're not inspiring to me or if I don't sense a connection with them I can easily let go of the opportunity to meet them. I won't go out of my way to meet someone just because they're famous. They'll have plenty of other people to mob them. Not everyone famous is influential in a good way, and I position myself to connect with people who inspire me with their attitude, tenacity, knowledge and wisdom. And I love to encourage them – everyone benefits from encouragement.

Connecting with purpose

I record short videos with leaders and entrepreneurs for the purpose of encouraging and inspiring others – and often to connect them and their message with a wider audience. For example, at the Neuroleadership Summit in San Francisco 2011, I was chatting with Kenny the Monk who had spoken at dinner, sharing a profound message about transition. Our chat after dinner was laden with more pearls of wisdom from Kenny, so I asked if he would mind having some of this conversation recorded on the iPhone video so that I could share this wisdom with others. He said, "Of course". I asked a colleague who was standing with us if he would record. As Kenny spoke about his brush with death and the clarity it gave him about living fully, I was so grateful that more people could hear his message.

Over the next couple of days at the Summit, I had a few other insightful conversations between conference sessions that led to short videos to share with others. Stuart Crabb, Facebook's Head of Learning, shared his insights with me on recruiting for 'innate curiosity and the ability to solve problems' and cognitive neuroscientist Jessica Payne shared excellent tips for brain health, particularly for entrepreneurs. Ironically, I was feeling quite jet-lagged as she shared from her field of study – sleep, stress, memory and cognition. Her gems were excellent and important to share because they make such a difference in our everyday connecting and living purposefully. Jessica shared three essential things for our brain, which she said is "your biggest asset":

- Managing stress – keep it moderate as stress hormones wreak havoc.
- Get good, healthy, nourishing sleep.
- Expose yourself to as much positivity as possible, because there is a lot of studies showing that "positive affect is key for healthy brain function".

Chris Williams, a director in NASA, was another insightful presenter and great company. I spoke to her after her presentation to thank her and because I was curious about her work, having always wanted to go to the moon. Having made a genuine connection, we spent time together over lunch and debriefing various sessions.

Sara Mathew, CEO of Dun and Bradstreet at the time, inspired me from the stage by sharing the highs, lows and humbling moments of her leadership journey. I met her later in the foyer and thanked her for her honest presentation and we talked for a while. I felt enriched by our conversation and was grateful that she was happy to share with viewers her encouragement to "dream big" and "be a learning leader".

I saw myself as the middle person sharing ideas between two sets of people. I could talk to globally influential people without being nervous because we were sharing a passion for learning, and I felt that I was privileged to be there and could learn and share insights with others who couldn't attend. What I was passionate about was what opened the doors to connecting with these leaders:

- I'm passionate about people.
- I'm passionate about encouraging people.
- I'm passionate about regional people or those who are isolated in some way whether it's geographically or socially, mentally or emotionally.
- I'm passionate about local businesses. Again it's people and community.

- I'm passionate about creativity. When I'm admiring the view, it's not just about the view. A beautiful view allows me to see a different perspective or a bigger picture and relate that to other aspects of life and learning.

It's good to connect with famous and influential people because we can learn so much from them and they have interesting stories. They have generally come to where they are because of the decisions they have made and the hard work they have done. They have insights and wisdom to share that they don't often share unless asked.

Many people don't share what they know because it is not rocket science to them and they don't know that people want their insights unless they're asked. The ones worth learning from are often quite humble. Let them know you really appreciate their insights – and their time.

So if we have the opportunity to talk to someone who is a leader in their field, we can benefit along with others in our world and we can give something back. If our approach is genuine, respectful and appropriate they are often happy to share. It is great if they can be appreciated for who they are as an individual, not as a persona. This is another great reason to connect – to appreciate them and acknowledge the effort they put into their work. Encouragement is for everyone.

Be confident, be brave and step out. Get out of your own way. Be about other people and something you're passionate about.

People who are new to fame or influence can be more difficult to connect with authentically. Perhaps they are coming to terms with the attention. They may have a sense of pressure and expectation from themselves and others. The may suffer from imposter syndrome, not feeling successful, fabulous or clever as they have been made out to be.

Jane and Michael Pelusey and I attended a function and travelled in the same vehicle as the winner of a reality television show. The conversation in the vehicle centered on his recent win and subsequent opportunities. There was an air of pretentiousness and we had photos together that we didn't feel inclined to share along with our other social media posts, as we'd walked away feeling a little uncomfortable. We realised later that it was the sense of a lack of authenticity, perhaps in all of us as we were part of the conversation.

If your world suddenly expands without you growing into it, you could well feel excited, but somehow not ready. When you look at the stories of what happens to people when they win the lottery, you see clear examples of what happens when your outside world changes dramatically and you haven't adapted to your new world on the inside, in the areas of your thinking, habits and beliefs.

In contrast, we met Matt Moran, celebrity chef and owner of Aria Restaurants who has worked his way to the top. We had a purpose in connecting with him as Jane and Michael had interviewed him earlier that day for their first Live Your Passion book, and then interviewed me over an amazing lunch at Aria for the second Live Your Passion book. Even though Matt was extremely busy, he responded to people wanting to meet with him in an unpretentious manner. People stopped to say hello and introduce their family to him and he graciously stopped to meet them. It was evident that Matt had grown into/earned his fame and was humble, unpretentious and approachable.

Something enabled him be the face of his business and still have time for fans. That also says something about his leadership and ability to build a team. He wasn't doing the too-busy and too-important routine to connect authentically with people who look up to him. If people are in the public eye they are looked upon as role models and must remember that. They are no more important or special as a human being than the others around them. With greater influence comes greater responsibility.

Leaders need encouragement too

I had the opportunity to unpack some phenomenal insights about leadership when I was on a high ropes course with some colleagues as part of a business development week with Dr Joanna Martin. I had almost accomplished my main objective to complete the course, especially the most challenging part where "80% of people fail". Perhaps it was my determined, rebellious nature that drove me to complete it. I said to Joanna that "I might be delusional, but I am determined". I chose to be in the top 20% before I even knew what the day involved. I knew that I wasn't as strong or fit as many of my colleagues, definitely not in the top 20% of fittest and healthiest, but I was determined. I won't be told I can't do something.

At the most difficult part I had pulled myself up a cable on an angle having watched people stronger than me slide back down unable to complete it. I pushed off as hard as I could to gain momentum and kept pulling hand-over-hand to maintain momentum. I'd realised from challenges earlier in the course the power of momentum – on the course, and in life and business. The last few metres pulling myself up the cable were agony; it was sheer willpower and the encouragement from another participant, Alan, who was above me that made it possible to reach the platform.

The next stage was to step through a course of stirrups that hung on ropes. I had to weave my way through without buckling at the knees or waist because I knew I wouldn't be able to pull myself up to continue. After congratulating me for completing the two most difficult parts, Alan sent me on ahead which was a simple walk along a 10-metre cable holding another cable above me for support. It looked simple and we had done previous stages like this, but I had spent all of my energy. I was really struggling, standing on the cable, trembling from head to foot from absolute muscle fatigue, far above the people down on the ground and far from the friends who had gone ahead down the flying fox. Alan was behind me, cheering someone else on at the stirrups, and I felt very alone and not strong enough. The pride and accomplishment of completing the hardest parts was quickly disappearing, as I felt suddenly weak and incompetent on the easier section that I no longer had the strength for.

I found myself part-way across and alone. The thought came to me that it's lonely at the top. I have noticed this emotion at other times in my life, sometimes following an achievement. People have cheered me on to do things, then when I'm done they would think I don't need encouragement. If they had thought of me or seen me they would think, "She'll be right. Kerrie is fine with challenges like that. She loves it and it is easy for her". After publishing my first book a friend shrugged and said "You do things like that" – very matter-of-factly. I was surprised that what was an enormous personal challenge to me looked easy to others. It had been a scary decision requiring focused work and feeling especially vulnerable as it was written from the heart. I'd taken risks – financial, emotional and relational – to publish it and let it out into the world.

I noticed how lonesome it felt at the top of the ropes course. This insight came back to me with increasing impact a short time later as I stood on the platform on the other end. My entire body was shaking and I felt completely spent as I waited for Alan to come across. As he was inching his way towards me, he called out "Kerrie!" I replied, "I'm here Alan", surprised that he seemed to need to know that.

He said my name again a few moments later to check that I was still there and I realised that he needed to know someone was there and that someone was believing in him to make it across. That was the wake-up call for me. I realised that I had thought of Alan as strong and capable and someone who did not need encouragement. He was older than me and super fit. It's not just me who feels 'lonely at the top'! How easily I expected that he had it all under control and didn't need my encouragement. Perhaps I was thinking that my encouragement would be taken the wrong way or rejected and thought who am I to cheer on someone stronger than me?

This is when I realised the expectation we have on strong capable leaders, that they just do these things and we minimise the impact that encouragement can have. I focused my attention on Alan, encouraging him to take step after step and helping him see that he was getting closer and that he could do it. We then zipped down the last flying fox to the end. Even though we were weak, we were buoyant with the sense of success, and during our five-minute walk back to the front gate we actually found the energy to skip part of the way, laughing and celebrating together.

I had so many insights that day, at various points along the course, but this one comes back to me so often. It's really been a key turning point in my understanding of my calling to be a safe place for leaders to stretch themselves to do challenging things and just be who they are without expectation. Simply encourage them and be there for them, celebrating their wins and cheering them on before they reach their next breakthrough. I've also learned that it's toughest just before the breakthrough. This is why we don't quit when we most want to. It's because the win is finally… almost… within reach! If you've completed 95% why not push through the final 5%?

Another moment where I saw encouragement making the world of difference was at the 2006 Melbourne Commonwealth Games. The women's marathon was coming to an exciting end with Australia's Kerryn McCann and a Kenyan runner battling it out for first place as they came into the stadium. As they entered the stadium side by side 100,000 people roared with encouragement. I only saw this on television but I felt the surge of energy as the crowd stood to their feet cheering loudly as Kerryn raced ahead to win gold by a long stretch. I remember the post-race interview where she shared the impact of the crowd's cheers lifting her and carrying her across the finish line.

I wonder how many leaders face incredibly challenging moments and just need the boost of encouragement and belief to get them through to their finish line or completion of their project.

Leadership isn't easy but it is worthwhile and we all benefit, so acknowledging, appreciating and respecting might just make a bigger difference than you realise. So, in the case of meeting Sir Richard Branson, I was appreciative of his contribution to the event that day and his inspiration for Australian entrepreneurs. I acknowledged his contribution to the book and our business journeys. I was respectful of his time pressure and mindfulness of needing to move, so when he put his arm around me and said "We will have to keep walking" I complied of course. If you have a rare moment like this, go with the flow.

While some moments with influential leaders might be an unexpected, highly unusual situation, others are extremely organised and surrounded by security, for example, if you're meeting the Queen or other royal guests. In a situation like this you'll have time to prepare and ask relevant organisers what the protocol is. All I can say on this is prepare. Know what you can about the situation, relax, be yourself and enjoy the occasion. Worrying about how you look and sound will take the joy out of it.

What we want from each other is to be more human. We need to be a safe person to be with. So be that safe person. Expect the unexpected – so then it's easier to be okay with someone else's story that is very different to your reality. Don't play it safe – be adventurous but appreciate the need for people to feel safe. When you feel safe with the right person you'll let them strap onto you and leap out of a plane with you. Safety and risk can go together beautifully.

COACHING CORNER

- Who inspires you?
- With what purpose would you like to connect with them?
- In what way could you contribute to their world?
- How could you encourage them, thank them and/or learn more from them?

Children and animals

It has been said you should never work with animals and children, but when it comes to talking to strangers they can be the initiators of some great conversations. My friend Penny Taylor from Port Hedland has shared some beautiful stories about her children, especially her young daughter, connecting with strangers. This has resulted in some great opportunities like going back stage at a show, to making people feel really special and reminding adults of how we can care for people. I remember Penny telling me about a day that her daughter approached a man on a scooter, kissing his feet because he couldn't walk.

A compassionate child doesn't think of hygiene or appropriate contact. She just loves freely, and reminds us to look beyond the dirt to see a human being.

Children often create new connections for us as they race ahead and connect without inhibition. Babies create new connections because strangers who may not be confident to connect with another adult are taken in by a cute baby and can prompt a question or comment: "How old?" or "So cute!"

I noticed when my son was born, complete strangers would pass me in the street and say "Cute baby!" Children open doors for us, but often people are embarrassed when they attract a stranger's attention or laugh too loudly or say something funny. We can observe children connecting without inhibition. While I am not suggesting that we interrupt people in conversation at restaurants (we may not have the cute factor), we can possibly step somewhere between their openness and our hesitancy to connect.

When you are out and about with your children, or your pet, don't be surprised if you find yourself in conversation. Notice that every conversation will go differently and notice what works in general. Consider how you feel when you say hello. If you're saying hello because you're happy to, or because you feel you should, you'll get a different response. The mood you're in will affect those around you, and therefore the response you get. You could take a friend who talks to strangers and watch their interactions and responses because sometimes you can learn by observing. When you begin to focus on how people interact positively, the more positive interaction you will get.

I spoke with a woman on a train in Sydney who had been a full-time commuter and was currently on maternity leave with a new baby. She shared with me that she was really enjoying the train travel now and the conversations with people that she'd never had before when she was in commute mode. She was planning to go back to work soon as her husband had started working from home to take care of the baby. Having conversations on the train was now something she's looking forward to continuing. I know that she'll be commuting and connecting with others, especially those who she relates to – women with babies in prams and other professional women who have a baby at home. These kinds of connections not only pass the time pleasantly, but can be a source of great encouragement and other positive outcomes.

My cousin Tania shared the following story with me recently:

> I went to the medical centre for my daughter's six-week needles. While waiting I got a coffee at the café there. The owner came out of the kitchen to greet me. She was very friendly looking, and after taking my order asked how old my daughter was. We started to chat about the six-week needles and she asked my daughter's name. 'Anastasia' I told her, pronouncing it the way we do in Russian (Anastaciya). The café owner asks if I'm Greek, as it's a Greek name and I pronounced it correctly. I explain my Russian heritage and she explains her Greek heritage. It then turns out we both married men with an Irish heritage. Further chatting we discovered that we grew up in the same suburb in Sydney! This was the highlight of my day as I miss living in Sydney and seeing my baby's pain from needles isn't pleasant.

This is such a great example of how a baby can open the door to conversation. Most mums won't mind someone enquiring about their baby and giving them the opportunity to connect. I'm sure it wasn't just the highlight of Tania's day, but also the lady in the café who went the extra step beyond just taking a coffee order. When you're away from home or in an unsettling environment – awaiting needles can easily cause anxiety – it's so wonderful to connect with someone who knows about a place or people that puts a smile on your face. It's the joy of shared connections, shared memories.

Young children, who haven't been taught to fear or judge, are interested in the world around them and their curiosity causes them to approach someone. Children don't make judgements. They don't mind if you are young or old, your size, skin colour, clothing, gender or mobility. Sometimes they'll comment on these things and embarrass their parents, but their comments are usually without judgement. Rather than teach children what we fear, we can teach them what is appropriate, what is positive and what is safe. I have seen people teach their kids to be afraid of the dentist, and for whatever reason they are passing on their own fear and not thinking about the impact of their words and actions.

When I worked with a dentist I saw parents coming in, sitting in the corner while their child was in the dental chair and making comments such as, "The mean old dentist is going to come in with a needle and you have to sit really still". Personally I find this ridiculous and wonder why you would make it harder for everyone and give the poor child nightmares. Instead, you can be more conscious of your words. You might say that the dentist is there to help or that they will fix a painful problem and make things better.

Try seeing the world through the eyes of a child. Maybe sit in a park or swing on a swing and watch the world go by without rushing or making something happen. Wonder how a child would see another child or an old man shuffling by. My friend Sarah Kelly shared the following:

I love how children become instant friends at a park. I took my three young children to a park for a play. I like playing with them, but their energy for play always outdoes my own. I am always thrilled when there are other children there too because my crew just include them instantly in whatever they are doing. On this day I watched them include two other children in their adventure. As I watched I noticed the other children's mother sitting on the opposite side of the park. I decided that if it was easy for our kids to become instant friends, then perhaps we could too! So I approached her and simply said, 'Don't you love how kids can become instant friends'. She smiled at me, and we chatted easily about parenting, schools and relationships. When it was time to go, I felt like I had made a new friend too.

For someone who is shy and wanting to talk to strangers for business networking, or just growing in confidence, start by going for a walk in the park where you are likely to pass people with dogs. You wouldn't start a conversation about a human's grooming, but you can compliment a dog's appearance and the owner will be proud of their pet. Comments such as "What a beautiful coat", "How old is he or she" and "What breed is your dog?" spring to mind. I don't think you need to be a huge dog fan to connect with people over their pet. If the dog's tail is wagging say, "That looks like a happy dog".

We can also learn from a dog's approach to life. Every outing is the best one they have ever been on. Every person they see gets their tail wagging. Dogs love life and love eating, love being with people, and love being in the moment.

Look - *for the positive in the situation and a compliment might be better than questions.*

Newcomers

Any organisation, networking group or club is made up of two or three types of people: the newcomers, the old-faithful and the people in-between. We may not have become old-timers but we have all been newcomers.

One of my favourite occasions to talk to strangers is in an organisation or group you know well. There may be people attending for the very first time. Newcomers if you will. For someone to actually come to a new organisation can be a bit nerve-racking. They're taking a big leap to actually join. They may be thinking, "I want to make friends" or "I'm really interested in the topic". Or it could be as simple as, "I want to get out there a little bit more". They decide to front up, they've taken a big deep breath and put themselves out there. There's nothing worse when you're taking that big leap and no-one seems friendly. The people may be friendly but they can be wrapped up in their own issues, work or other friendships. However if they can't break through, they may never come back again. They may not get the courage to do it a second time.

At the same time how many organisations are looking for more numbers? I think it's all in the welcome and the connecting with people. People might like to go to a stamp collector's guild or a church or a library function. But no matter how interested they are in the subject, if there's no connection they can feel disappointed and alone in the crowd and they may not come back. They may perhaps go and find a similar organisation somewhere else. It might reiterate their beliefs about not fitting in or not being able to connect with people. If someone at the organisation was a little more insightful and aware, then there could have been a more successful welcome.

First let's talk about people who are going to these things. Sometimes there is an expectation on the organisation to be friendly and welcoming. And sometimes newcomers arrive and people might not realise that they are new. They might be busy or preoccupied, which is a shame. They might have expectations of someone that are unreasonable. You might have expectations of a particular person welcoming you, but they don't. You could jump to conclusions that perhaps that person is a newcomer as well and also be trying to work out who do I talk to here?

So from a 'taking responsibility' perspective, as the new person, we can just be brave enough to go to the function in the first place and then use that bravery to take the next step. That is, introduce yourself to some people, perhaps with a comment or question like these:

- "It's my first time here, is this what usually happens?"
- "Can you please show me where the bathroom is?"
  (Or the office et cetera).
- "Is there somewhere I can get a cuppa?"
- "I'm new and a little uncertain as to what to do or where to go or who to talk to".

You may join a group or a couple of people who are chatting because they look great to be with, but that could be a bit of a stretch at first. If you are standing on your own, it may be better to talk to someone else who is on their own. You can make them feel more comfortable and by doing so, you will too.

For people who are part of the organisation, whether you're on the welcoming team or not, we can all be on the lookout for someone who seems a little uncertain or is simply standing on their own. When there is an organised welcoming team there might be a function associated with that role, such as offering a brochure or info pack, but it's best if it doesn't feel like a job. People like to connect with people who want to be there. It's good to be on hand to welcome people, whether you are assigned to it or not.

Have you ever received a warm greeting at a function followed by the cold shoulder because they have done their job? That can feel quite disheartening. Obviously, if you're the welcome person, you can't hold everyone's hand all night, but you have a great opportunity when they first come in to introduce them to someone else. It could be something like, "Mike is standing over there and he'd love to say hi to you".

Find out who else is great at welcoming people or connecting with those within the room. Then, as guests arrive, connect them with potentially like-minded people – "Jane, have you met Suzie?" Then quickly follow-up with something that Suzie does for a living or has achieved lately. That will get a conversation going. By breaking the ice this way a good connection may occur. If that doesn't happen, at least both parties can confidently enter conversations with others.

If you are one of the welcoming team, be aware not to over-welcome, which can make people uncomfortable. Some events have an over-the-top welcome at the door with very enthusiastic people. There can be too many people welcoming. A quiet person who is overwhelmed by crowds can look for another door because they don't want to go through the 'wall of excitement'. Some organisations need to know that not everyone wants to feel like the life of the party with a lavish greeting. It's about being appropriate and aware of the people you're talking to.

Extroverts get their energy from being in a crowd like that and introverts don't. So you don't want to be draining them and making them feel uncomfortable. I think when someone at the door is saying:

"Hi Jane! How are you?" or "Hi! I'm Kerrie, nice meeting you", you don't need or want someone behind you doing exactly the same right there in the moment. Just have one conversation; even if it's very brief, one quiet and focused conversation can be so much better than lots of rushed ones.

It can be so disheartening turning up to a new event only to find people don't seem to even care about you being there. A pivotal moment occurred for Lyndon and I on our honeymoon. We were excited to see a church across the road from our hotel on the coast and decided to go to the evening service. It seemed that the people inside only welcomed each other. Even after mentioning that we were on our honeymoon they looked disinterested. They didn't seem to want to know anyone who wasn't a local. You would think it's easy to talk to someone on their honeymoon – "When was the wedding?" or "Where did you come from?"

What it did for me was put a determination in my heart to never do that to someone else. I think if you grow up in the same place, particularly a small town, you know virtually everyone. I lived in the small New South Wales town of Gilgandra. I went to the Anglican Church and Lutheran school, so I rarely walked into an environment where I knew no-one. I felt alone sometimes, but I was never a newcomer.

My honeymoon experience made me really aware of what happens when people are completely new to an area and don't know a single person. In the church we visited, Lyndon and I were obviously together because we were probably holding hands. Maybe people were confronted by talking to two people at once. I know, having been a very shy person, I couldn't handle a conversation with more than one person. I did find that very intimidating. But you would think, and this was my expectation, that someone would be happy for us and think it would be really nice that we came to their church. So it just made me very aware of welcoming people, whether it's in church or retail stores. It's just about welcoming people to the space that is familiar to me, but not them.

In retail, people generally want to look around and then ask for help, but if the shop assistant hasn't made them feel welcome, they won't ask. You have to stay open, be friendly, and let people be who they are whether they are introverted or extroverted – just be okay with that. Recognise that everyone is different. We can't have a one-size-fits-all welcoming policy or script.

Let's look at a networking event where you think, "I don't need to connect with a real estate agent because I'm not selling my house". By being rigid like that, you limit opportunities to connect. Be aware it may be the key to introducing you to the mayor or a builder who you want to talk to or a lawyer or someone whose child goes to your childs' school.

I was a newcomer at Western Australian chapter of National Speakers when Jane and Michael Pelusey took me in 2013. I felt very welcomed by everyone there, and although I met lots of people Rabia Siddique was the one who I've connected with most since then. We only connected briefly, but we heard each other speak for 5 minutes. She connected with me on LinkedIn. I don't use it as much so I asked her if she was on Facebook and we connected there. As I was writing this book Rabia was completing hers, called Equal Justice. When I came back to Perth I invited Rabia to attend an event I was speaking at and attending with Jane.

On this occasion, I was the newcomer and Rabia connected with me. That has opened my world up to her world, her military background and her hostage experience in Iraq. So we learn more about the world when we connect with people who are from a completely different world.

COACHING CORNER

- What event could you attend in the next week or so?
- What focus will you choose? (Eg. learning from others, making people feel welcome)

Old faithfuls

Sometimes, we just need to be reminded that we can take people for granted. We often spend so much time focusing on welcoming new people that we neglect the old faithfuls as I call them. We don't value the people who show up week in, week out, making the cups of tea and coffee for everyone. Organisations run because someone's mopping the floors, stacking chairs, making tea and coffee, and doing all those bits and pieces. We need to be just as pleased to see them as well. Sometimes it just means raising our awareness again and choosing to be grateful for those people because it is about acknowledging them and saying, "I see you and you matter". It's about giving people that respect of being a fellow human being.

Organisations can get obsessed with membership and new members but then forget about retention. There's that cliché about having the front door open but the back door's right open as well. Someone might be an old faithful and you might have that embarrassing sense that you should know their name as they've been in your world for a long time. It could be the guy who sweeps the floor after an event and you realise that you've been taking him for granted. You then think that it's too late to go and start a conversation now because it kind of shows up the fact you haven't before. The fact is: you haven't before so you might as well just own it and acknowledge them for being such a great contributor to the organisation or it's awesome that they're still coming after so many years. You can say you're sorry you haven't spoken to them before. That will make them feel appreciated.

Better late than never is what I think. It's good to get started. I went over and met a neighbour who lived across the road and down a bit and said, "Hi, I'm Kerrie from over the road … ". She replied, "Oh I'm sorry I haven't come to meet you!" I said, "Oh, that's okay. I had it on my mind to pop over and meet you for a while".

She added that she was coming to say hi when I moved in and asked if it was earlier this year or last year. I said it was two years ago and she was so embarrassed it had taken so long. Then we chatted. Even though it was an awkward moment for both of us, it was totally okay and we are chatting now. I did not move in waiting for the neighbours to greet us. I could have gone and met them all. As time permitted, I met the neighbours one by one. Unfortunately, I met one of my neighbours because the dead cat in their driveway was my son's. Then we chatted about the trip he was going on. It was a pity we met under those circumstances. The point is we met, we chatted, and it was a better late than never conversation.

It's a shame we have to wait for special occasions to go talk to strangers. Just because it's Halloween people suddenly have permission to go and knock on the neighbour's door when they couldn't before. Of course it doesn't mean everyone's ready for it, so you still could be catching them at an inconvenient moment like you could any time. Maybe door knocking is not your thing, but any day of the year we can smile at someone in the street and say hello.

The old 'drop-in' isn't done so much anymore, possibly because everyone is so busy. I also think its partly that because everyone has mobile phones you can just call ahead. For me, I love the spontaneity of dropping in, after calling – "Can we chat this afternoon?" "Yeah sure! Just have to get this thing out of the way so give me 10 minutes". I guess 'dropping in' can be dropping into someone's world in various ways such as dropping in with a chat on Facebook or a phone call or text. Any of that can just make someone's day. Of course it's important to gain permission immediately – asking "Do you have a few minutes?" or "Is it convenient?"

People often say "We should catch up" so getting the calendar out and looking at dates to schedule it certainly sorts out who is sincere and who isn't. Some people are insincere and just say "Let's catch up" to everyone without thinking. So if you say, "That would be great! I would love to catch up with you – this weekend suits us", you might break through a bit of a wall that they might have up and make a deeper connection. Everyone has a desire for connection and we're built for connecting with others, but it's not always easy in our busy lives.

Speaking different languages

There are so many opportunities to connect with strangers and we can have a memorable encounter with anyone, even if they don't speak the same language. It is clearly more comfortable to speak your own, sticking to what you know. Let go of the need to connect with people in your language – from where you stand. Step into their shoes. Find other ways to connect. Be relaxed, happy to make mistakes and misunderstand each other. A sense of humour and positive attitude will take you further than eloquence. People will appreciate that you are giving them your attention and extra efforts to connect and they'll increase their willingness to communicate.

There are many ways we can communicate without words. Sometimes it will just entertain you for a little while, teach you something new, or give you a sense of contribution or connection with another human being that enriches your life. Or theirs. As you might have realised, you can have an impact on others that becomes evident in their life after you have moved on. Just as there are people you can think of who've influenced you and you may have no way of finding them and thanking them.

Even on the other side of the world, language doesn't have to stop people connecting with people. My Dad shared these stories with me from one of their trips when he would have been dressed in his very Australian-farmer-style:

> *We stepped onto a train in France and there was a big French-African lady with a little girl, watching us get on and she laughed, looked out the window laughing, looked back at us and laughed and put her hands up like paws, like a kangaroo, and said "kanga-roo", but she didn't speak any other English. We sat with her, and Jenny showed her photos of our family. The lady then picked up a big bosom in her hands and pointing at the photo, as if to ask, "Did you breastfeed these kids – are they yours?" It was a hand signal and photograph conversation we had with a lady who didn't speak English.*

While that was entertaining, Dad's next story is a great example of being able to satisfy his curiosity around "How does this work in another country?"

> *"On a quiet French railway station there was a workman wandering up and down. I spoke to him but he didn't speak English. I wanted to know*

what the measurements were on the side of the train. He stepped it out and indicated that, without saying a word, this was axle measurement. Then he pulled a key out of his pocket and opened the door of the engine and invited me in by hand signal and indicated for me to sit in the seat. I looked at the steering wheel and thought it was unusual for a train to have a steering wheel. He pointed to the speedo and indicated, "Turn the wheel this way and the train goes slower and this way goes faster". I understood.

There was a button on the floor and I asked him "Accelerator?", wondering if he might know this word. No, he didn't understand any words, but he indicated going to sleep with his hands together, eyes closed, and started making a whistling sound, the first sound I'd heard from him. I responded, "Dead-man?". He excitedly said, "Ah!", indicating that it was the safety device commonly called a 'dead-man's switch'. If the driver goes to sleep and he doesn't hold his foot on that button the train will automatically come to a stop. It will start to whistle first to wake him up and then the brakes will come on if he doesn't push this button".

So Dad's curiosity was satisfied and the Frenchman was happy to share what was commonplace to him with someone who appreciated it.

Sometimes the most profound moments can occur in the least expected places, when the most common way of communicating is unavailable. This is when we connect human-to-human and it's so beautiful because it's such a surprise.

Cycling with friends through Cambodian countryside beyond the tourist-filled temples, we came out of a jungle and into a small clearing where we saw local women and children foraging for food. We stopped to see how they were digging for root vegetables and scooping tiny fish from puddles into buckets as we waited for our local guides to catch up. There was no common language, but our Singapore-based Japanese friend Masami Sato squatted down with one of the women, curious about their work.

The lady responded to Masami's curiosity and started explaining with her own language and hand-signals how various underground vegetables grow horizontally and vertically. We were interested to see how people lived in the country as we were on a study tour of social enterprises with Masami's philanthropic organisation, B1G1, looking at how our businesses can change lives beyond imagining.

The following story from Julie Woods, also known as That Blind Woman, is another beautiful example of connecting regardless of communication challenges.

> When you're blind everyone is a stranger! Even people who are familiar to you can come up and say hello and you don't know who they are. Then, I thought about my trip to China. After taking many publicity photos on the Great Wall of China, my husband Ron decided to take a wander on his own, leaving me with our guide. My guide then chose to leave me for the toilet, and I found myself sitting blind and all alone on the Great Wall.

> This is not how my visit to my second wonder of the world was to be. How could I turn this bad moment into a great moment? Then I had a thought, maybe I could give a copy of my book away on the Great Wall of China. Just as I was fumbling through my backpack to retrieve a copy of my book, our guide returned. By this time a crowd had gathered around me.

> One of the members of the crowd began speaking to our guide. "They want to know about you", she commented. "Where do you come from, how long have you been blind?" Perfect, the ideal opportunity to give my book to someone who is interested. It turned out to be a local Beijing family who were visiting with their 22-year-old son. As I outstretched my arms, I held my book out for one of them to take it. It met instantly with another pair of hands, this time the 22-year-old son who we learned had recently graduated from Beijing University with a degree in Japanese. At this moment I was

able to introduce myself using my schoolgirl Japanese and explain that this is where I had learned the language.

As the book met his hands he exclaimed, "I am so rucky!" (that's Chinese for lucky!) He then went on to read the cover of my book, not in Japanese though, this time in English. "How to Make a Silver Rining — 8 Keys for Adapting to Extraordinary Change!" (that's more Chinese this time for Lining). We continued chatting through our guide and just as we were about to leave the young man said, "Your t-shirt say That Blind Woman. Should say great woman!" Wow — to which I replied, "Great woman on Great Wall!", and we all laughed.

What a magical moment for me on the Great Wall of China. Just because I am blind and in a foreign country where I don't speak the language, it doesn't mean I am unable to have meaningful interactions.

My husband returned 30 minutes later, despondent and a little flat. He informed us that he got further up the wall he felt lonely so he decided to turn back. I just smiled to myself as I reaped the reward for talking to a stranger!

On another trip I was making a bouquet for the airport staff in Bhutan due to our plane being delayed for three hours. I made it as I sat in the airport waiting for our plane to finally take off. I asked Ron to write "Have a nice day" on a piece of paper and I attached it to the bunch of flowers. When the girl came back over to give us an update on our flight departure I handed her the bouquet. Even a blind woman could see the smile on her face. "This is for you", I announced, pushing the bouquet to what I thought was towards her.

When Ron and I handed over our boarding passes 20 minutes later another young female staff member came over and without any warning said

"Thank you so much" and nuzzled into my chest for a stranger snuggle! Boy. I felt uplifted through my actions and I'm picking they did too. Can you imagine my feelings about Bhutan at that moment? It was magic!

As you can see, the Right People to connect with can literally be anyone. If you are only looking for the 'important people' the serendipitous and significant moments could pass you by.

Relax - *be ok with having misunderstandings or making mistakes.*
Enjoy - *laughter doesn't require a shared language!*

RIGHT PLACE: ANYWHERE

Let's explore the locations where connections can occur. Everywhere from social media, networking events, traveling, shops and the middle of nowhere. I met a girl in Port Hedland airport who told me about driving from Perth to Port Hedland and the intense loneliness that sets in when you have over 17 hours alone in the car. On a trip like that any human being you come across is delighted to stop for a chat.

This chapter will show you that no matter where you are, whether on your everyday commute or in the most random locations you can create genuine connections if you're open to adventure, Interested In Others and willing to Start Small.

Social media

I have SO many social media stories of wonderful connections that could fill a book. A great example could be that you found this book through social media.

Somehow I connected with Kylie Bartlett from Geelong when she started a Facebook account a few years ago and was adding friends. I was one of her first 10 friends and there were a few messages between us. I had been on social media for a few years and generally only connected with people I knew or who had introduced themselves. Kylie and I clicked, (no pun intended), and appreciated each other's posts so we felt a sense of connection. We agreed that social media was about being social and there are real people on the other side of the computer. One day I picked up the phone and rang her. "Hi, it's Kerrie Phipps your Facebook friend". She said, "OMG you actually rang me".

Keeping in touch on Facebook made it easy to let Kylie know when I was speaking in Melbourne at a publishing event and she came in from Geelong. She has since been to my Conversation Events in Melbourne and I've been to several events that she's spoken at in Sydney. We've both been enriched by not just the connection with each other, but by sharing resources and networks. This is an example of many of my online connections.

I connected with Jill Hutchison on Facebook through a mutual friend. It was one of those connections that you are not sure how it started, but you saw a comment somewhere and felt you were on Facebook for the same reason. And that is to connect and inspire and encourage and connect with like-minded people. Not long after we'd connected online I was planning to come to Perth for a breakfast with Sir Richard Branson, thanks to my Perth friend Terri Billington inviting me. (How my world has changed since then! Thank you Terri!)

Jill and I had a new connection based on my upcoming Perth visit, which included a book signing event at Borders Bookstore. This was because of a phone call I made to a stranger, the marketing manager at the store, and the enthusiastic Stefan hosted several events with me in the bookstore in March, May and November 2010.

I mentioned to Jill in a Facebook chat that we were on our way to Brisbane because my father-in-law was unwell and in hospital. After less than two days with him, he passed away. Because Jill and I'd been in conversation over the preceding days I updated Jill. Our online connection suddenly changed from her interest in my Perth visit to being a caring compassionate friend, who shared the most practical supportive advice about dealing with the first few days of loss and what to expect. I had never experienced the loss of a family member before, not even a grandparent, as all my grandparents have lived into their mid-90s. Jill's father had recently died and she shared her experience and what her mother went through, so to have access to that kind of knowledge and wisdom to support my family was really valuable and extraordinary. I met Jill in person about two weeks later in Perth and our friendship has grown. I've stayed in Jill's family home on subsequent visits and love seeing her inspiring journey unfold.

On social media we are connecting with people. Remember that it's another human being on the other end. You wouldn't walk past someone in the street and throw your business card at them and expect them to say, "Thank you so much, yes, I'd love to follow you!" We wouldn't do that in life and certainly would not get that response. In the old days of Facebook, when you clicked add friend, a box would open and you could send a message. In 2011, they removed that function and now you have to actively click on the add message. And more often than not, depending on the individual's settings, it may go to the 'other folder', which many people are unaware of. Facebook hint – it's worth checking your 'other' messages from time-to-time, found next to your 'inbox' in faint letters.

I was aware that people were being encouraged at marketing and other business events to add friends on facebook, but no-one was reminding them to send a personal note and interact online. This means a lot of people are randomly clicking 'add friend' to build the number of connections they have, yet not seeing their business or network grow offline.

It is incredible to have the opportunity to build friendships with people before you actually travel to a new location. In preparation for a trip interstate I would connect, interact and ask questions of people who were doing something similar. I would engage in small but meaningful messages, which means more than just liking things. Someone who just clicks the 'like' button and doesn't share much on their own page isn't inspiring or indicating a potentially rewarding relationship. You can't get on Facebook and watch what everyone else is doing without sharing a little bit of yourself. (It's called stalking.) It is okay to be very private on Facebook but don't expect others to engage with you. The Golden Rule applies here as it does offline – "Do to others as you would have them do to you".

Some people are on social media without any purpose in mind, not all that different to wandering down the street without any real purpose. Choose to live purposely online and offline. If you don't live life purposefully you may blame others for what is going on in your world. Anyone can live on autopilot. Fulfilling your potential doesn't just happen. You create the life you want with the words, choices and people who are aligned with your purpose.

One of the issues with social media is that you are talking to people using only words on a screen. There is no voice tone or body language so it is easy to misunderstand. There is a tendency to read between the lines and misinterpret the meaning of a comment. With a quick glance at a screen we can make assumptions about what people mean and it's worth taking a moment to clarify.

What assumption are you making?

When someone tells me they never make assumptions I have to bite my tongue. Or challenge that idea. The human brain makes assumptions constantly based on the information available. We need to be open to new information and to change our thinking. Just because someone didn't share your post doesn't mean that it didn't make their day. Perhaps they loved it and wanted to share but didn't have time to do anything but a quick 'like'. If you're making a negative assumption, you can just as easily make a better one! That voice of negativity in your head doesn't speak the truth, so combat it with something more empowering.

We have all heard of someone's mum or grandma who has just learnt how to text and sent something like, "Sad news today. Aunty Lois passed away. LOL. Mum". It is important to remember that we have a unique language that regular Facebook users are familiar with. This language could be completely misunderstood or confusing to others. Make sure your mum knows that LOL generally means 'laugh out loud' and not 'lots of love' – both positive messages but for different scenarios!

COACHING CORNER

- What assumptions have you been making that you'd like to challenge?
- What is your purpose for connecting online? How does it vary to suit different audiences?
- What opportunities do you have this week to more consciously connect through social media?
- What does Starting Small look like in the online world?

Networking events

How do you feel about networking? What does it mean to you? My definition of networking is connecting with people. I love people and I love learning and growing. When all three come together at a networking event, it's magic! Many people are not comfortable in a networking situation, whether it's a school carnival or meet-the-Prime-Minister event.

Labelling and letting go

To enable you to let go of pressure, anxiety, a sense of inadequacy or anything that will prevent you from connecting authentically, here is an exercise to help you clear that and choose your focus. It is important to identify what the emotion is that is present as a backdrop to your thoughts, for example, if you are thinking the people attending the networking event are more professional and educated than you, notice how you feel and when. Is it a sense of inadequacy or is there another emotional label you would put on it?

A child falls over, hurts their knee, has a cry, gets up and continues playing. They express that emotion and move on. As we grow older we find that expressing is not so socially acceptable, therefore we suppress the emotion and hide the angst or feeling that is still there. An emotional response is a normal and natural brain response. Regulating emotion is something you choose to do. A very useful method is to label it and let it go; a habit that is easy to develop.

Once you have labeled or given a name to the emotion you are feeling, it is like it feels acknowledged and can sit quietly to the side. The limbic system in your brain is a bit like a child saying, "Look at me! Look at me!" So when you acknowledge the fear, anxiety, pressure, uncertainty, it is like you say, "I know you are there, I hear you. I want you to be quiet now, because I am choosing to focus on something more empowering". An example of this might be "I am feeling uncertain, but I am sure I wouldn't be the only one (choosing to be certain about something) so I will choose to be relaxed and welcoming to help others connect and relax."

Making it practical

If you're struggling to do this in your head – 'park it' on a post-it-note or scrap of paper and bin it. Write a couple of words to sum up the situation and the emotion attached and let it go from your thinking as you let it go into the nearest bin. And 'pick up' or choose the focus like 'relaxed' or 'open' or 'adventurous'.

So in order to help others feel more comfortable, bearing in mind the golden rule – to do to others as you'd like them to do to you – you might offer someone a drink and ask them how they are hoping to benefit from the event. A question might be what do they like about these events, as they could be thinking about what they don't like about them. It is important to keep a positive focus and think about what you like about networking events. If you focus on what you like you might be able to think more positively, for example, this is great venue, it is a helpful organisation, what an opportunity to learn something new. If you have some answers to these questions yourself that is a good start. Having answers to the questions you ask others is useful.

Being in service to others takes the pressure off you. If you make people feel more comfortable, confident or happy within themselves, they will remember you more positively. Remember, "People don't care how much you know until they know how much you care" – John Maxwell.

It is not so useful to be the most knowledgeable in the room but you will be remembered if you are caring and genuine. Then they are more likely to want to know what you know. Being knowledgeable may put you on a pedestal but it can be isolating if you can't make authentic connections. If someone leaves your company liking themselves more, I count that as a huge win.

Other useful things to keep in mind are:

Be yourself!

If you're stressed and frantic before opening the door, then you switch to immediate composure, the stress will show through … and who wants to talk to someone who doesn't seem authentic? Being yourself is so much more fun and relaxes those around you. Let go of the stress before you walk in.

Focus on others

Do this in your questions and attitudes. One of the best things I learned when I began coaching was, if you're nervous, you're thinking about yourself. The best way to lose your nerves is to turn your attention to someone else – think about making others feel comfortable.

Get out of the comfort zone!

That's where the best discoveries are made. When you've left your nerves at the door you're free to take opportunities you may have missed before. Meet the influential and the famous – they are people too – who appreciate conversations with genuine connections. You never know where a conversation can take you.

"He who walks with the wise will become wise" – Proverbs 13:20

Remember to also acknowledge and converse with people who are serving you. There's much to be learned from others regardless of their day job. And they are worthy of your appreciation and respect. They are fellow human beings with hopes and dreams too. I would not have met Sir Richard if I hadn't connected first with the venue employees.

Keep the focus positive

You'll always encounter negative people. Don't go down that path with them! Look for the best and tactfully share a positive slant on the subject. If that's not possible, give them a moment before gently leading the conversation elsewhere – to a topic that will put a smile on their face.

"A man never likes you so well as when he leaves your company liking himself"
– Unknown

Imagine that you are so happy to be there and enjoy making others feel welcome. If you focus on that you'll find it becomes true. You'll go home feeling great and others will remember you, especially important when they're ready to do business.

A few quick practical tips

- Go to an event with someone you know and separate shortly after arriving.
- Offer someone a drink, find yourself a job – walking around with a platter is a great way to warm up and meet people – but don't hide behind it.
- Make an effort to remember people's names and use them.
- Be clear about your business and what you love about it, so you can answer succinctly when you're asked, and you can inspire people to want to know more.
- Collect more business cards than you hand out. Send a note of thanks or invitation to meet for coffee if appropriate. Enjoy seeing your network grow, and your business and personal life flourish!

Following up with emails

It is great to have a system for keeping in touch and following up with people you meet at a networking event. For quality connections personalise follow-ups. For example, the same happy birthday message or the same copy and paste on every Facebook friend's wall will become obvious and lose its impact. After a networking connection I may make a note of how or through whom we connected and something else I would like to remember about them. If I drop someone a line to say "great to meet you", it has to be more than just a one liner. I might have a link to a resource that I mentioned at the time.

I could share useful information or acknowledge them for something I learned from them in our conversation. People can have a "What do you want from me" suspicion. I often just connect and would like to stay connected purely for the potentiality of what might happen in the future. Connecting because I respect them, and without attachment, I welcome them to my world. A question often raised is how much time do I have to give to strangers who I have just met. I am not suggesting you go for coffee with everyone you meet; it comes back to listening to your intuition.

In this world of email blasts and automated replies, we have become numbed to true connection. Keep your electronic communication simple and authentic and avoid the copy and paste bulk email. Just because you have been given a business card it is not your right to add them to your list. Add them to your contacts with a few key words so that you can find them easily by a quick search later. If you see an article that may be of interest to them, this might be another point of connection that demonstrates your interest in them.

COACHING CORNER

Easy connecting:

- Go to a networking event with someone who is happy to go separate ways when you arrive.
- It is easier to talk to one person than multiples of people, which might feel like you're in front of a job interview panel.

Public transport

Another momentary meeting happened early one morning between train stations in Sydney. I was going into the city for training and my book, *Lifting the Lid on Quiet Achievers*, was in the final stages of layout. I sat on the peak hour train with my MacBook on my lap, checking the relevant pages and sending an email to my publisher. A gentleman sat down beside me and I said good morning. I remember saying that I wouldn't normally be working on the train. In fact I don't usually catch trains as I work from home in the country. I closed the MacBook as our conversation ensued as he was curious about my book as he was interested in regional Australia.

I responded purely out of respect. If someone with headphones in their ears had sat beside me I would have smiled (if I'd caught their eye), perhaps said good morning and gone back to my work. It felt like the fair and respectful thing to not be using technology next to someone who wasn't. Our conversation unfolded as we connected with smiles and basic greetings.

Successful conversations are absolutely a two-way street. I give a little, the stranger takes it and does something with it, or lets it go. If he takes it, he gives back with a question or comment, then it's my turn again. We share the experience. We're both giving each other the time of day, the present moment, instead of a multitude of other things we could be doing – staring out the window, thinking something through, being tired, flicking through emails, playing a game, or actually getting work done. What you're doing, working on or thinking about, might be of some interest to a stranger you talk to. You won't know if someone is interested in talking to you unless you say, or ask, something that will open a door to a conversation.

I discovered that the gentleman I connected with was the CEO of the Vincent Fairfax Family Foundation, which I wasn't familiar with at the time. I did Google the foundation later that day as I was curious. Geoffrey left the train with the comment, "I'm going to tell them at the office about you". I discovered online that VFFF are big supporters of regional, family and youth programs so was not entirely surprised by the connections that followed …

A week or so later, I received the following email:

Hi Kerrie,

Geoffrey White recommended that I get in touch with you, saying that you would be a great person for me to know. I am heading up the School for Social Entrepreneurs in Australia. We started earlier this year with a school in Sydney, and we launch in Melbourne early in 2010…

If you are interested in learning more about us, I'm happy to have a conversation. Indeed, if you are ever in Sydney, I would happy to meet up also.

All the best,

Benny Callaghan

I then received a call from Jocellin Janssen, CEO of the Country Education Foundation of Australia with a similar message – "Geoffrey recommended that I call you … Will you be in Sydney again soon?" It was just good manners to have and be open to a conversation, or at the very least, a hello. Look for opportunities to serve others in small ways. You'll never know where things will lead.

When Jocellin called me I mentioned Benny's email and she was delighted as she had worked with him previously. The three of us met for coffee at Circular Quay, along with my colleague and friend Roland Hanekroot. I loved hearing about the work they were doing and when Jocellin asked me if I could help get an Education Fund going in Dubbo I said I don't think I'm the right person, I wouldn't do it justice, but that I would think about it as I'd probably know the right person.

Not long afterwards I spoke at a business women's lunch in Dubbo and shared the story of a simple good morning on the train and the events that followed. After the lunch, Lyndsay Lowe came to see me and said, "Tell me more about this Country Education Foundation". Knowing of Lyndsay's work and connections in education I said, "Oh my goodness – you're probably just the right person!" Lyndsay became the driving force behind establishing the Dubbo Country Education Fund, and it wasn't too long before Jocellin was in Dubbo launching the Fund at the Commercial Hotel. I was really sick with the flu but I sat up the back of the event so grateful that I'd said good morning that day on the train. I'm sure they would have connected with someone in Dubbo at some stage, but the Dubbo Fund was launched in 2010 and many students have received grants for tertiary education support since.

Another day, at another city train station, I overheard someone with a problem, not a big one but an annoying one. I connected with the problem because I'd had the same issue a week or so before. I connected with her frustration and empathy drove me to connect.
I asked permission to interrupt by saying, "Excuse me for overhearing but I'd had the same issue and can show you how to fix it if you like". The girl let me into her world for a few minutes to help her solve her problem. A deep trust wasn't needed but she did accept my help because I wasn't threatening in any way. She could have said, "I'm fine thanks, I'll figure it out", and been independent. There's nothing wrong with that, but by being interdependent her problem was solved more quickly.

I assumed that they wouldn't mind. My desire to connect and help others is greater than my fear of rejection. My sense of connection with her and understanding her frustration was bigger than the possibility of her rejecting me so I didn't think twice. It isn't pleasant when you offer someone your help and they say, "No, I don't want your help". I generally assume the best of people and if they're not friendly I know it's not about me. I don't have to take it personally. If I feel that they may not accept my help that makes my approach a little gentler. You don't just barge in and say, "I'll fix it".

People are observing and you don't realise. People like happy people. Tone of voice is really important, but it is something that is really hard to do naturally and be conscious of it. However if you choose your attitude, your tone of voice will follow. I genuinely like people. People are more important to me than work. People are the priority for me. I might be in a hurry, but I would still say hello and have a brief chat. Sometimes when I say good morning, people in big cities will look surprised because they will be thinking, "Do I know you?" or "What do you want?", and perhaps concerned that they'll be delayed. When time is precious people don't want to give it away to just anyone.

Attitudes change on different days of the week, times of day, special occasions and even different trains. The train that includes the airports is different to the average commuter train. When people get on the train at the airport stations, I feel a responsibility to welcome them. I might be the first person they have talked to other than the immigration or customs person scanning their passport. They may feel a bit lost or jet-lagged and might appreciate a friendly word and face. I create the setting that it is okay to ask a question. I have a thing about making people welcome. Welcome people into your space, be an ambassador. People matter and they need to be made to feel welcome. So whether it is shops, church, city, country or at business networking events, people should feel welcomed.

This determination may have come from when I was shy and I would have liked to be made to feel welcome. I know how hard it is to walk into a place on your own. It is hard to walk in knowing you are alone, as I shared in my introductory 'confession', so to be welcomed by an unofficial 'ambassador' is refreshing and often quite a relief.

Judgement

We judge people because of what they are wearing. We judge on people's posture and gait. The other day I was walking/jogging down a street near home and saw a man wearing clothes that were ripped and he wasn't walking a happy walk, so I chose to run on the other side of the road. If I had said good morning straight away when I had the opportunity I would have known whether my initial judgement was right or wrong, but I missed the opportunity. I should have acknowledged him when he caught my eye as he passed by. My uncertainty means I could have missed one of those incredible connecting moments, but it also meant that I could have regained some certainty and felt safer. Because our brain instantly decides 'friend or foe', and a neutral expression generally says 'foe', we cannot even give the 'assumed foe' a chance to smile and perhaps relax us.

I was on a platform awaiting a train at 7.09am. I'd never been on that train line before, so I arrived a few minutes early and sat alone on a bench. Minutes later, a well-dressed lady walked past me and looked so classy. I thought, "Wow!" and wanted to say "I love your suit! You look fantastic!" She was a little far away and it would be weird to call out. I might embarrass her if the whole platform heard, so I thought I'd tell her if she was on the same carriage.

As I was thinking this, another well-dressed woman sat on the bench next to me. I said good morning! She turned to me and said, "Oh, hello", a little uncertain. I asked, "How are you?" She replied, "Well, thanks", still a little uncertain. "Do you normally travel on this line?" I asked her adding, "I haven't been here before". She said, "Oh yes, every day. Where are you from?" I said, "Dubbo". She relaxed and said, "Hence the friendliness!" I explained that I was in Sydney for the few days between our coastal holiday and ANZAC Day and my grandfather's 95th birthday. The conversation continued as we stepped onto the train, so we sat down and talked all the way into the city.

I like to discuss general life topics, like family, places, sunshine and other everyday stuff that has people feeling equal. Because I believe we are. If the conversation begins with "What do you do?" it can quickly alienate someone who feels inferior. If we can connect on 'ordinary things' then when work, business or education comes up, it's not such a threat.

If you are introduced to someone with a great title it can be easy to feel intimidated. If you encounter them as another conversational human being first, then their role or experience is more likely to be interesting and less threatening.

This particular lady and I were discussing Dubbo and when she was last there. I followed up by asking if she'd been there for work or with family or friends. She replied she was a lawyer back then, but was now in banking. When I asked her where she worked now, I realised that she is in the same building as Hans Kunnen at St George who I'd met and kept in touch with over the past year. It was lovely to make that further connection. That conversation with her prompted me to send an email to Hans and reconnect. He was not in Sydney that day, but we met for coffee a month or so later and shared another insightful, encouraging chat.

Travel

Travelling is one of the best ways to connect with strangers, whether you're going across town or across the county or, less frequently, across the world.

If you're not a leisure traveller, I recommend a trip just for the opportunity to see new sights and meet new people. I know that a lot of people reading this might travel a lot, and it's easy to get into habits of isolating yourself so you can get to your destination with little delay, perhaps getting work done on your way, or sleeping, which is fair enough.

But don't deny yourself the opportunity to connect with others at various times. I have had many plane trips where I thought I'd just write, or sleep. But I've said a polite good morning and the door is open to conversation, which might take place immediately, or as a meal is served, or as we're coming into land.

Sometimes the conversation has continued for most of the flight to the surprise and delight of both of us. The important thing is to be open and go with the flow. Again, it takes two. Or sometimes three or four.

Without realising until now, I've developed a bit of a plane boarding routine. As I sit down, or if my fellow passenger sits down after me, I say hello and take a few minutes to settle into my seat and put my bag, books and magazines away. I give my fellow passenger the same opportunity. I choose a relaxed moment, but if I have made the initial connection with my hello it's easier to then pick up the conversation again when you're comfortable.

They might be the next one to speak, but if not (and if they're not hiding behind a paper) I might ask, "Are you just going as far as (insert current flight destination here) or further on today?" This question is an easy one for me because I travel two or three flights from home to an interstate destination. I'm well aware that others might be going somewhere further than the next stop, and possibly somewhere quite interesting.

Another question, when I realise I'm next to a frequent traveller, is "What the most interesting (or random, or best, or most amazing) place you been to?" This can unlock a great conversation as people can share some great memories that will put a smile on their face. People love to share memories of significant people and places. And if you make a connection in your thinking, i.e. you think of someone or somewhere and wonder if it might be a shared connection, just ask! "Do you happen to know" or "Have you ever been to ...". For example, I have met accountants and entrepreneurs from all over Australia and New Zealand and have asked, "Do you happen to know Anna Cochrane? Or Leanne Berry?" It's amazing how many times I get a yes! It may not be a significant conversation, but the brain is always happy to make a connection and we leave with a smile on our faces, pleased with the sense of an increased bond.

A surprise connection occurred as I was preparing to leave Papua New Guinea, browsing in a gift shop in Port Moresby Airport. I said hi to a girl I saw wearing a shirt similar to the style I often wear and said something like, "Nice shirt! I like that style". She was so excited, and I didn't understand why until later. We had a brief chat there in the store and discovered that we were booked on the same flight to Sydney. She introduced herself as Malina and shared that this was her first international trip. She was going to a nurses' conference in the USA and was so relieved to have made a new international friend already.

When I entered the boarding lounge a little later, I noticed her excitedly pointing me out to her friend and learned that she had referred to me as her new friend. After take-off I went down to where she was seated on her own and I joined her there for a few hours. She told me about her nursing work, her family, the devastation of her father's murder and the inspiration he had been to so many people through his leadership and church conferences that supported many remote communities. The connection we shared was quite extraordinary and I was amazed at her resilience, faith and determination to give her younger siblings the opportunity to be educated.

She suddenly said to me an hour or so into our conversation, "I would like to give you this shirt" (the one she was wearing). I told her that was lovely but to keep it, but she wanted me to have it, as it was the thing that first connected us in the airport store and she wanted me to remember her. I said, "Well would you like my shirt? We can swap when we get to Sydney if you like". So we did – once we landed we went to the bathrooms, handed our shirts to each other over the cubicle walls, and left with a parting hug and a photograph of us in each other's shirts. I don't think I've ever been offered the shirt off someone's back, or given the shirt off my back, but I won't forget it.

Showing hospitality to a traveller

My Dad was collecting his mail from the box on the highway a few kilometres from the farm when a tourist on a motorbike stopped for a quick chat. Dad invited him to come down the dirt road to the farm and have a cup of tea with him and mum. Emile, on holiday from Belgium, wrote in their guest book, "You must come to Belgium and I will be your host and guide". My parents thanked him for the kind offer but didn't expect to be travelling to Europe.

At that stage, married over 20 years, they'd never left Australia and didn't expect to. However, Dad had been involved in the re-enactment of the 1915 Coo-ee March from Gilgandra to Sydney, marching for three weeks in 1987. So when he was invited to 'complete the journey' in 1993, and commemorate those who served and many who lost their lives on the Western Front, they began to plan a trip to Europe. Dad referred to Emile's note and made the phone call. "Emile, do you remember a farmer from Gilgandra? And Emile said, "Ross!! You are coming to Belgium?! I will be your host and guide!"

Several weeks later, my parents arrived by train at Oud-Heverlee in Belgium and went to a public phone to call Emile. Unsure if the sound was a ring tone or a busy tone, they asked a lady passing by, "Do you speak English?" She replied, "I teach English!", and introduced herself as Sandra. She drove them to Emile's house, where they discovered he wasn't home. She put a note on his door, "I am looking after your guests", and left her number. Sandra rang her relatives and friends to come for afternoon tea to meet these "strange Australians". Generally, over there when you say Australia they hear Austria, which is far more familiar to them.

Mum has kept in touch with Sandra from time-to-time. She wrote to mum several years later and shared some of the challenges she'd faced and then these words, "There are two things that keep me going – I am determined that my children will have a good future and second, I saw the faith you had when we met at Oud-Heverlee station". Mum says, "I didn't know that we were expressing a lot of faith, but I guess she saw something in us that encouraged her".

Emile was a wonderful host and guide from the time he picked them up from Sandra's and he drove them all over Belgium, showing them many wonderful places. Your hospitality can be repaid in bigger and more significant ways than you can imagine. Dad's offer of tea and a visit to the farm resulted in a wonderful time in Belgium, and Sandra's hospitality opened the door to great encouragement in her own life.

Because of the re-enactment component of their trip, at times Dad was dressed in 1915 clothing looking very Australian and somewhat out of place among modern Europeans. One afternoon they were on the London underground train, with regular commuters heading home, reading the newspapers. As mum tells it, a drunken Irishman with a bruised face and broken teeth boarded the train. He saw Dad and called out across the carriage, "G'day Croc!" likening him to the iconic

Crocodile Dundee. Dad would be the last person to judge someone on their appearance and happily chatted about the reason for their trip.

A young Pakistani man nearby said to them, "You have just broken the unwritten rule of the underground". Mum asked him what that was. "You do not speak on the underground", he replied. All the people who had their heads buried in their newspapers looked up, grinning, and went back to them chuckling.

While the rule is 'do not speak' people actually enjoy a more memorable trip when there is a positive interaction.

In a recent article, "Mistakenly Seeking Solitude" published in the *Journal of Experimental Psychology: General*, Professor Nicholas Epley and Juliana Schroeder demonstrated that commuters who engaged with others reported a significantly more positive experience, even when they had expected a negative result. You may have noticed this yourself as you've been reading this book and looking for opportunities to connect with those around you. There are often more smiles than expected!

Connections come easily when you travel

On a recent flight from Singapore to Siem Reap in Cambodia I sat next to a lady who lives in Singapore and was going there for the first time to have a weekend with friends, travelling around. I slept for part of the trip, but chatted with her at the start and end of the journey. I was so tired I wasn't feeling well. I saw her again in the toilets at the airport and she looked like she'd seen an old friend. It's amazing how when you're in a new country and you don't know a soul, even someone you don't know well can be a delight or a relief to see.

A few days later I met Billy Gorter in Siem Reap. He founded This Life Cambodia, whose educational programs we support through Buy One Give One (B1G1). I overheard two words of his conversation with Paul Dunn as we travelled by bus to a regional village. As we walked through the village, I walked a little faster to catch up with Billy and asked him, "Did I overhear you mention World Youth?" He said he had and I asked, "Do you happen to know Sandra Groom or Barbara Anderson?" We were both amazed and delighted to discover mutual friends who we've both spent quality time with through coaching and philanthropic work.

When I shared this on Facebook later that day Barbara (in Sydney) and Sandra (South Coast) were amazed to see that I was in Cambodia for the first time and on the first day of the study tour met one of their friends! This delight could easily have been missed if I didn't JUST ASK! If your brain makes a connection – in this case World Youth as I'd known of Sandra and Barbara's significant involvement in World Youth International – it's worth asking the question that comes to mind.

This also led to an incredibly profound insight that came out of my conversation with Billy. He asked how I'd connected with Paul Dunn (chairman of B1G1) and Masami Sato (founder). I shared with him about hearing Paul speak in Sydney and seeing the overview of how B1G1 gives you the ability to connect every business transaction with an act of giving. I explained how with each book sale, we gave a fruit tree for food and income for a family in Rural India, and with each speaking engagement or coaching program I delivered, we were able to fund entrepreneur training or education projects in Cambodia.

I shared with him that Lyndon and I, for as long as we can remember (at least 20 years) have had a dream of being able to be "generous on every occasion". This was a quote of the Apostle Paul and an aspiration we'd held onto that had seemed so far from reach as it sounds like massive wealth is needed to be generous on every occasion. As I spoke to Billy I suddenly saw that because of B1G1 we can be, and we are being generous on every occasion that money comes into our business. With every invoice paid, we give a small percentage. We had discovered that every time we give it makes a difference, whether it's as small as giving one child water for one day, or one teacher a wage for one month.

The impact of this insight was significant as I've always felt that I wish I could give more, and I suddenly shifted from what I haven't done yet to what I have done and what I can do. I was greatly encouraged and thankful for the conversation with Billy, his simple question followed by his listening ear that allowed that insight to emerge.

Shops

It's amazing who you meet in shops. Sometimes it's the staff, or maybe you're the staff, but sometimes it's the other customers you're standing in line with or browsing nearby. If you want practice at talking to strangers, here's a great place to start. Commenting on an item of interest or beauty can ignite a conversation, as can paying a compliment or sharing a dilemma. In which case, it's better to comment on it in the context of the store being popular or the staff being "run off their feet" than a negative tone of complaint.

I was discussing this book with a friend I hadn't seen in a while, who doesn't talk to strangers often, and he told me of his most recent encounter. I thought it was a great example of a 'shared dilemma', which is a common connector. He was standing in an aisle in Bunnings and overwhelmed by all the choices of gadgets and a man nearby made a comment about how challenging it was to find something. This was the beginning of a conversation and they helped each other find what they were looking for. Not a life-changing conversation, but an encouraging one, and these little collaborations and small connections help us feel less alone in the world.

Another friend, Beth Tickle, shared her enthusiasm for talking to strangers with me and I noticed another shared dilemma being the connection point.

> *I talk to strangers with a purpose in mind. I mean, I don't go rushing up and talking to every stranger I see. But sometimes I'm attracted to people who I imagine might have similar values to me. Or an opportunity arises when literally there's nothing to do but talk to strangers. Some people feel uncomfortable with it. Obviously, it doesn't work for everyone, but I strongly recommend trying. Sometimes it is literally a serendipity experience.*

> *For example, the other day, I was in this GIANT line at the bank during my lunch hour. The lady next to me and I started a conversation. We chatted and jokingly complained about the queue together which made us feel better. I found out she was from Narromine, a nearby town. I thought she would appreciate our magazine (Central West Lifestyle). We talked about Narromine and she gave me some ideas for the magazine and I gave her a recent copy of it and we both left very happy. That's how talking to strangers can have a positive outcome.*

You have to remember that not all people are comfortable with talking to strangers, but we all have a desire to communicate in differing amounts, and people are often quite flattered that you would want to speak to them. And if there's a challenge or dilemma unfolding, you could stand there and tweet your annoyance and achieve nothing. Or you could connect with someone nearby and help them manage the stress and alleviate your own as you experience the joy or simple connectedness of being with another human being.

In adversity – hard times and traumatic events – when connection really counts

Running up the train station steps just after peak hour I noticed a young woman leaning over and she vomited. I was coming up the steps behind her and I did have a moment of will I just keep going and pass by, because vomiting makes me feel the same way and she would be very embarrassed to be doing this in public. I wondered how far she had to go to get home and if she needed help.

Sometimes it is worse when someone is compassionate and you feel horrible because you can start crying when you've been holding it together, but it can feel very lonesome to be sick and on your own. I reached out and put my hand on her shoulder. "Are you okay? Do you need anything? Do you have far to go?" She waved me away and said, "I'll be fine", to which I replied "I hope you feel okay soon".

Even though it is horrible and you wish you were out of sight, it might help to know someone cares. We all need to know someone cares. I also hope she had someone at home to commiserate with. She could be mortified that a stranger interfered, but I would rather make that mistake than holding back from caring when I had the opportunity to do so.

Another less than pleasant moment I'll never forget took place a little closer to home in one of the shopping centres in Dubbo. I was out the back of a retail store, using their staffroom to wrap a gift for someone, and my friend Tiffany was manning the store on her own. She called out to me, "Kerrie can you come, I don't know how to help this lady". The lady was standing at the front of the store, standing still looking very uncomfortable. As I came closer I could see she was quite unwell and looked like she might faint. I asked her if she needed a chair. She didn't say anything. I knew something was not right but didn't know what it was. She could barely speak. Her first words were, "I don't know what to do?"

In that moment I was grateful for my coach training and learning to wait for a response. I am okay with uncomfortable silence and waiting for people to say something. I asked her what she needed. I waited again for a reply as she was clearly ill, uncomfortable, and embarrassed. I'm not sure which way it happened but she told me she needed a change of clothes and then it hit me: the realisation and the unbelievable smell. Still unmoving, she asked if the store had a pair of tights. I looked back to Tiffany who brought a pair over.

I asked Tiffany for her staff keys so I could take the lady to a more private bathroom. I took her there and then went up to the department store to buy her some underwear. Then I did another trip to get a bigger pair of tights. I saw myself in the mirror and internally encouraged myself to hold it together because of my weak stomach. The lady might feel worse if I gagged, or worse, threw up. She started to worry about her husband not being able to find her. I said I would look out for him as I went back upstairs to get a bottle of water for her.

As I came out of Tiffany's store with a bottle of water from the staff fridge I saw a man near the escalator looking concerned and said, "Are you looking for a lady who isn't very well?" He said he was and I said, "She is down here", and he came with me. She had exited the bathroom and was sitting on a seat out the front. They were both really grateful that I had been there to help and they tried to give me money. I let them give me money for the water, to pass on to Tiffany, but I felt grateful that I was able to help her and I was there for her. I felt happy to be inconvenienced, and was glad I was there because it could have been more awful for her. I was also grateful I could give what I would want if something similar thing happened to my mother or grandmother in such a humiliating situation. I never thought I would write a book that included a poo story, but there it is.

When I saw myself in the mirror I was also asking God to help me not vomit and stay composed. It was one of those moments when you know you were meant to be there. That knowing contributed to my sense of gratitude. I was glad I was available and it did make me a little late to pick up my son, but when I told him how I'd been able to help a very sick lady he didn't mind. It was great that I was able to share the experience with him, as I know he is compassionate and would understand. It's also good to share with children that it's not all about them, just as it's not all about us as adults, but that any one of us can put our plans on hold for a little while to help someone in need.

Are we available for those moments when we're 'in the right place at the right time' when our help is particularly needed? Will we rise to the occasion?

I wonder if people who stop and help with big things are people who stop for little things? I wondered this as the news of the Boston bombings spread across our news channels. Along with the horror, there were many stories of people rushing into the danger zone to help and many running away. This is not to judge those who ran away. In such a situation there are many unconscious decisions to run one way or the other as everyone saw the situation uniquely. No two brains are the same and everyone had a different version of what happened, the sounds they heard, the things they saw, and all the information around them they unconsciously processed in an instant. The thing that emerges in moments like this is a common connection that we are all human beings. Status, gender, ethnicity and age do not matter when someone needs help.

Jane and Michael Pelusey were in Bali at the time of the 2003 bombing. They connected with strangers in adverse conditions. Having gone to bed early they were woken by a very loud noise and then heard another one. Thinking it was a gas explosion they went outside where the locals said to stay inside the compound. Information was non-existent and no-one knew what was going on, just two kilometres from the tragic event. Within an hour a man who was staying at the hotel stumbled into the compound. He was bleeding from cuts and abrasions so Jane, being a nurse, started dealing with the injuries. As she picked glass out of his arms and legs he relayed his experience. He had seen the suicide bomber blow himself up. He ran out the back instead of out the front where the second bomb was. He survived but relived his experience over and over. There was nothing they could say to help. It was a matter of sitting with him so he wasn't alone. In traumatic situations you don't have to try to fix it, you just have to quietly connect.

Sometimes there are no words, but it's enormously helpful to just be there. In any kind of disaster when people are rocked by shock, grief and horror there isn't much you can do but be there for someone. A friend and I came across a car accident not far from home, where it appeared that the young driver had fallen asleep at the wheel and gone off the road and hit a tree front on. The steering wheel, along with the rest of the front part of the car, was pushed up against the driver so he was trapped. All we could do was wait for the ambulance and keep him calm. Just being with him and telling him we were there helped him focus on our company and distract him from the panic of being trapped. You might feel useless in some situations, because you don't have the training of a paramedic, but your presence is sometimes an enormous support.

In reverse if something happens to you, let people help you. We are so good at being independent, but we might get through a situation more smoothly if we had accepted or asked for help and allowed someone to give the gift of caring.

I was driving back from Wellington to Dubbo, a half hour road trip after work, and I broke down and it was getting dark. I pulled over, popped the bonnet and I couldn't work out what was wrong. I decided to leave the bonnet up and hazard lights on and chose to sit in the car rather than try and flag someone down. I was wearing my bank uniform, a classy little skirt and fitted jacket, and thought I didn't want to attract the wrong type of attention. But I thought the bonnet up and hazard lights would attract a practical, helpful type of person like my Dad. I was in the car for half an hour thinking where were the

people who would pull over and help? This was before mobile phones were commonplace. I prayed for someone to pass who was non-threatening and had a mobile. A car pulled up on the other side of the road and the window wound down. It was a girl's voice, "Do you need any help? I have a mobile phone...". That girl wanted to feel safe as well in her assistance, so she'd pulled up opposite me so she could speak from inside her car. I was very grateful to have my specific request answered. She drove me back to Dubbo and I rang my husband on her mobile on the way home.

Whether your challenge is an inconvenient dilemma or a traumatic, life-changing event, it's often the little things that make the biggest difference. Small acts of kindness can have an impact that is never forgotten.

I first met Hans Kunnen, a senior economist from St George, when he visited Dubbo a few years ago and spoke at a business breakfast where he mentioned his experience on 11 September 2001. We've discussed it more since then as he was so impacted by the kindness of a stranger and I was also impacted by his story. When Hans was in the middle of a crisis in a foreign land he made a connection with a stranger because of his consideration of her.

Hans had been visiting the World Trade Center for a National Association for Business Economics (NABE) conference and was at a breakfast meeting when they heard a distant thud, like an explosion. Lights, chandeliers and tables shook. People started screaming, left all their belongings and ran for the exit. Hans was in the first tower to be hit by a plane. He was scheduled to fly back to Australia that day but couldn't get upstairs to get his luggage and passport, so evacuated as most people on the floor had done, not knowing what had happened. Once outside, he heard a low flying plane and looked up to see it slam into the other tower, so to get away from the city he went down to the Staten Island ferry.

What initially connected Hans with this stranger who became an incredible support to him was a small act of service. He recounted, "As people crowded onto the Staten Island ferry to escape the horror I offered my seat to a lady, but she declined. The same lady then tried to put on a life jacket and knocked off her earring. I picked it up and gave it back to her. We got talking. She had seen my name-tag from the conference – Hans Kunnen, Sydney, Australia – so she asked where I was going. I told her of my plan to seek refuge at a church and she invited me to stay with her family". At Leslie's home he tried to contact his wife in Sydney, but the phone lines were not working. He recalls,

"After about four hours we got through, much to Suzanne's relief. She had seen the second plane hit the towers on TV and knew I was directly underneath".

It was another week before people were able to get back to Australia and Leslie and Rod accommodated Hans for a few days until he moved to a hotel near the consulate and airport, "They fed and clothed me and tried to keep activity as 'normal' as possible. We visited parks with their young son, we ate out at a diner and visited Rod's work". Such simple moments of connection that could easily have been missed in the chaos and uncertainty ... offering his seat, picking up Leslie's earring ... and her noticing his name tag and enquiring. These are everyday things. Simple things can open beautiful, timely doors of opportunity and friendship.

Community events

Another great way of connecting with others is at community events. It could be a running festival, a healthy life expo, fundraisers, school fetes or market days. People are often wandering around, relaxed and open to new ideas and new people, so you can find these places easy to connect.

I was recently at the Dubbo Farmers Markets and was chatting with Susie Collett at her famous Lime Grove produce stand. I stepped back to let her connect with others who came near her table and overheard the most delightful conversation. She spoke to a young German woman who was working in the region on a travel visa, and her parents who'd come for a visit. Susie's response to her story was, "Oh how wonderful for us that you've come here!" I can't think of a more welcoming statement. This joyful expression was so honouring, as if we are the ones graced by their presence, not how lucky for the German family to be able to visit us. Local pride is great, and we do love that people come to visit because we know they'll love our region too, but it is wonderful for us to have visitors come. I'm sure it made their day – it made mine and I simply overheard it.

Every conversation is unique, and because of the special nature of community events, anything is possible. Standing at a display or produce stand it's easy to say to someone nearby, "Wow, isn't that interesting" or beautiful/creative/different, or "Have you seen anything like this before?" You could learn something interesting, share something of interest to others, and perhaps make a connection that lasts a lifetime. If you feel like you'd like more conversation with someone you've connected with, you can always ask, "Hey do you want to sit over there, maybe grab a coffee and tell me more?"

You might have a tendency to be a little closed off to people if there are lots of things on sale, but remember – you can say "no thank you". I think so many people don't engage in conversation because they're afraid of being sold to. Learn to say no in a way that doesn't make the person wrong for offering or 'trying to sell' but that keeps you focused on what you want.

It's like saying hello to people with no strings attached, being unattached to the outcome of a conversation, and if the other person you engage with can't be unattached and tries to lure you in, just smile, say "no thanks" or "not now" and be okay with your decision. Their opinion is their business. At the end of the day, they'll remember the conversations that were more involved – whether that's an argument or a delightful sale – but a brief interaction is not going to stick with them. If you want to be remembered, be memorable in a positive way, or just keep moving on.

When you feel drawn to connect with someone, just do it. Don't let fear or hesitation or lack of convenience get in the way. On ANZAC Day 2014, as I marched with my grandfather, I saw hundreds – maybe thousands – of cameras pointed our way. Of all the photographers there was one I asked as I marched by, "Do you have a card?" He said, "No, do you?" And I said no, but he keyed my number into his phone as I called it out and he texted me. I had no idea who he was or if he'd be happy to share, but we'd connected. Within an hour of the march being over, my ANZAC day photographer friend Jonathan Alt and I had shared an emotional connection through a few brief text message reflecting on the day. He texted a request/offer to take photos of Grandad if he'd be happy to sit for a portrait. His photos of Grandad and the conversations they've shared have been really special.

We arranged this photo shoot for the same day as one of Grandad's favourite events, the AMP Retirees Association luncheon, where I had the privilege of being their guest speaker. He also drove us into the city and photographed the event.

Seeing Jonathan chatting with Grandad and hearing his stories as he clicked away, I was so inspired. Photography is clearly Jonathan's passion, along with stories of mateship and courage. Jonathan created a treasure for our family, because of a momentary connection that we both made the most of.

At an art gallery opening a few years ago, where art works and their admirers were spread throughout several rooms and an outdoor area, I was on my way out the front door when I noticed a man with a really happy smile. I don't remember if he was speaking with a group or just one person, but his smile literally shone across the room. I said to my husband, "I just have to say hi to him before I leave". Lyndon, who'd been ready to leave for a little while, said "Okay, five minutes". He told me that he'd already met and chatted with the man I'd pointed out.

I can't remember my exact words, but my thought was, "I just have to say hello to you before I go. You have the best smile in the room". I know it sounds a little ridiculous, perhaps too forward, but I am a firm believer in saying what you think – if it's positive and helpful. Of course people can be really taken aback by this approach, but if you're confident in what you've said, you can respond to their surprise with another comment like, "I know that's really forward, but I thought it was worth sharing. I really mean it". And you can be confident – it's your opinion or experience so no-one can tell you that you're wrong. People will sense your authenticity and relax – and possibly laugh – which is okay. You can laugh too. Laughing at yourself is totally okay, and freeing.

I chatted briefly with the artist with the great smile, who I initially didn't realise was an artist. I had already met his wife Suzie, and so the connection with the two of them had begun. Lyndon and I, discovering that they were new to town had dinner with them soon after. Apart from the fact that we enjoyed their company, we're keen to welcome people to town and understand that it can take time for people to connect and feel part of the community. As time went on, we realised that this artist and his artist manager wife have an extraordinary story – actually they have countless extraordinary stories that span the globe.

I often connect with new people to help them settle into the community and I don't expect to hang onto the relationship – unless we all really click – but my intention is to help them connect with whoever it is who will become their friends. In this case that included us, and we've grown a lovely friendship that has been a support to each of us through various challenges, everyday life and exciting days too. The artist with the fabulous smile is Tim Gratton, who is a traditional fine artist, a world champion artist, known for his body art, his own brand of non-toxic body paint and many well-known advertising campaigns and creative projects. Suzie is an events manager and artist manager (which is how she first met Tim) and has raised well over half a million dollars for charity. Suzie and Tim are currently transforming Dundullimal Homestead from a nearly-forgotten old property to one of Dubbo's best tourist attractions.

Tim Pankhurst, Dubbo PhotoNews.

They have expanded our worldview in many ways, and our appreciation and skill in art. We've been in Tim's art classes and see the world, and trees and people and landscapes with curiosity and appreciation. I see a sunset and wonder, "How could I paint the light and shadows, those mountains, these trees?" I can't go for a drive now without seeing scenes I imagine painting and wondering, "How could I describe that exact colour?!" I met up with Tim and Suzie one afternoon downtown and noticed he was studying my face intently. His first comment was about my new haircut, but he kept looking at my face and then asked me if I'd sit for a portrait for Australia's most prestigious portrait award, the Archibald Prize. What an honour – and a great experience, but the afternoons in the backyard swapping stories with them are most precious.

They're both big fans of talking to strangers as many of their extraordinary stories have come from small moments of connection. Like Tim's train trip many years ago when he offered a beer to another traveller, which started a conversation that changed his direction, literally, and opened up doors that led him to becoming a highly trained, professional artist who has now taught many students around the world.

Cafés and food

One of the most amazing young people I've met unexpectedly is Sacha. I met him at Vivo Café near the Apple Store in George Street in Sydney. I was with friends, and he saw us taking photos and came over to our table and offered to take a photo of us all together. Another inspiring young person there was Phoenix, a girl who knew Sacha from his inspiring presentation at her high school – where he had a significant positive impact on her life (and countless others).

Sacha, Phoenix and I spent the next couple of hours together, including an Apple Store visit, where I saw more evidence of his connection with people. The interest he takes in each person he meets is astounding and beautiful. As we walked back to Town Hall Station I asked if we could share some of our conversation with our friends online so Phoenix kindly recorded before the next train came!

At a Thai restaurant in Coffs Harbour many years ago (before Facebook) I was dining with my friends Lijana and Irissa and we 'fell in love' with our waitress, Miriam. We thought she was lovely in her service but noticed that the other staff were quite rude and impatient with her. So our hearts went out to her and we wanted to encourage her. As we walked towards the front door, I put my hand on her shoulder and said, "Thank you so much for your lovely service tonight". I touched her, as I wanted to emphasise our gratitude, and her response was immediate. She put her arm around me and expressed her appreciation too, clearly delighted and so encouraged. I was surprised by her enthusiastic response and felt compelled to offer to keep in touch by email – an opportunity she jumped at. She said she'd like us to meet her friend Karoline the next day, and that she couldn't wait to tell Karo about how I was so 'sympatico'.

This connection that could have ended that night didn't. In fact it resulted in the girls travelling to Dubbo to stay with us, spending time on my parent's farm, riding motorbikes in 47 degrees (our hottest day ever), then meeting up with us soon after in Sydney for a Hillsong album recording with over 10,000 people, then driving me down towards Canberra where they met friends of friends at a conference they dropped me off at, then finally meeting up in Canberra a few days later as I was there for a friend's wedding. That's where we said goodbye as they continued their trip around Australia, but we kept in touch by email. When my parents went to Germany a few years later Miriam and Karoline were delighted to welcome them and showed them around. We've since reconnected on Facebook. How easily those memory-building moments and friendships could have been missed, but for the moments of each of us stepping beyond our comfort zone to offer a connection.

Tim Gratton came back from the UK recently and told me another great opportunity that opened up when he walked into a restaurant that was full and the waitress asked if he would be happy to share a table with a man who was also on his own. Tim said yes, and had a great time talking to the man there – who later offered him life-time access to box seats at Wembley Stadium!

Outdoors

On the Central Coast of New South Wales, I was floating up and down on the waves at a protected part of the beach. A girl of about 17 was inching her way into the water and smiled. I commented that it isn't so cold once you get in. I said I enjoy the beach anytime because I don't get here often. She pointed to some houses and said she lived in one of them. The girl chatted with me about the beach and shared some local knowledge. She decided to go and play with her nephews. I thanked her for chatting with me and said that often young people don't talk to strangers. She said her mum always does and called her mum over. We chatted for about half an hour about talking to strangers. She felt comfortable talking to strangers because she had watched her mother doing it while she was growing up and had an awareness of connecting in appropriate situations.

Learning from locals

Another beach situation reminded me of the value of talking to strangers, in particular connecting with local knowledge. My son Ethan and I were in a shallow strip of water in Queensland between the edge of the beach and a sand bar and then the great expanse of water. It felt wonderful and looked gorgeous. An older man who was enjoying the gentle waves didn't connect with us at all even though we weren't far from him, until I commented to him about how wonderful the water was. He then told us not to go further up the beach because he had seen people swept out. I couldn't believe such calm-looking water could be so dangerous but he said people had drowned there.

I thanked him for telling us and he said some people don't want to know. I felt it was important to acknowledge his local knowledge. It was a lesson for me in appreciating local knowledge and understanding that things are not as they seem. I wanted him to know that his input was valued, as I imagine that sometimes he would be reluctant to offer the information because people might ignore him.

If you have local knowledge you might not share because you think it is everyday life but for someone else it is very helpful. As a local, be willing to share with people who seem new to the area. It is important if you are the visitor to seek out, acknowledge and appreciate the perspective of others, especially the locals. If you are giving out local knowledge, don't come from attitude of fear alone. If there are dangers to be aware of, share it with the safest options and positive attributes of the area so that you are not simply being dismissed as grumpy or fearful.

As the listener, if we are hearing someone's local knowledge and it sounds negative and depressing, you can steer the conversations to solutions or better options by asking them what they recommend. People like to share their recommendations as well as their fears. The hospitality we give can be so small and insignificant to us because it is our own world, our routine. But to someone else it can be life-saving information. How many times do we not bother to share local knowledge because we make an assumption that they might not want to talk to us? He may have had previous negative experiences, but we really don't know.

A couple of years ago my family and I caught the ferry from Nelson Bay to Tea Gardens. Ethan and I were walking along the foreshore looking out at the river. On the edge of the river, we saw a man about 10 metres away. We stopped and watched to see what he was doing. He saw us and called out, "Have you had fresh oysters off the rocks?" He offered a couple oysters and we hesitated. I didn't know how hard it was to get them and was thinking he was giving me something of great value. I also hesitated because I wasn't sure if I liked oysters but I didn't want to put Ethan off. So I took one and swallowed it. Surprisingly, Ethan put his hand out for one as well. Not many 12-year-olds have a palate for oysters but Ethan certainly does. We chatted with the friendly man about oysters and where he lived.

It wasn't a big conversation, but it was a lovely one because we met someone who was in his element and sharing the joy of one of his favourite experiences. The chance meeting increased my son's appreciation for fresh, natural food. It was a novel experience for us, but it was normality for him, and our appreciation for it increased his enthusiasm. Your story is normal to you, but it could be quite interesting or inspiring to others. We could have glanced at him and kept going, minding our own business and not letting him see that we had been watching him. But it was a lovely spring day and we were happy and open to connecting.

You could make the assumption that if someone is outdoors that they are on a day off and we shouldn't interrupt them, but there is an opportunity for connection because we are both enjoying the great outdoors. We are both experiencing the same space, the rain, sunshine, clouds. We can take that loose connection and make it a better stronger connection, perhaps just for a few moments, but it can make your day, teach you something or open a door to a greater opportunity. Being outdoors is often out of their normal routine, so they may be relaxed and less rushed because they have chosen to take this time out. In that setting, people are more open to a hello. You are sharing the space, like a national park, so there is a sense of connection.

I often cycle with my son in the mornings as he goes off to school. One morning I went a little further with him, which opened up a new connection and my inspired thoughts. He waved to an older gentleman on the side of the road going back towards town. I asked Ethan if he knew the man and he said, "I just wave to him and he waves back. He feels special then and I do too". That is the essence of my "Do talk to strangers" philosophy. Make someone's day. When you acknowledge someone, you place value on them. You don't know their story; you don't know how much they might need a smile or an acknowledgement. You probably may not realise how much you need it sometimes too! We all love to know that we've made a difference somehow. A smile is an easy way to do this.

We parted ways as Ethan was turning right to complete the trip to school and I rode back, catching up with the walker we'd waved to. I rode past slowly and said good morning and then pulled up beside him and said, "I believe my son usually waves to you". He said "Oh yes, I often see him". I told him what Ethan had said and asked if he saw many students smiling and waving. Charles (we introduced ourselves) told me he thought society was less friendly these days and supposes it is progress. I couldn't help but share that I was writing a book to help us progress to a more connected world. We stood on the side of the street for the next few minutes chatting about where we were from and found that he knows my parent's neighbours well. Charles said with delight "Well you learn something new!" about the value of talking to strangers. ☺

Perhaps I might be good at talking to strangers because I've discovered that there's so much I don't know! Besides just enjoying the feeling of giving and receiving smiles, we love making new connections in the brain – not just the social world.

I have so much to learn, and I need help in navigating this big world, and I've learned that you don't know if you don't ask! Curiosity makes connecting with strangers easier. Being humble makes it easier too. If you walk through the world feeling like you know it all –heaven help us. I've been there and the pressure is intense! Friends – if I ever stop reaching out, asking questions, feeling I've arrived, please slap me. There's a huge difference between confidence and arrogance. Confidence says, "If I don't know I'll just ask as someone will be happy to help me".

So, want to join the fun this week?

Do talk to Strangers ☺

Step 1 - Smile and wave 👋

Step 2 - Call out good morning to at least one person a day. If you don't see anyone in the mornings, get out for a walk, or park the car further away from the building you're heading to, so that you have more chance of seeing people.

Step 3 - Take note of how you feel – what have you learned about yourself and/or others?

Step 4 - "How are you?" – ask it and mean it – express genuine interest
in others.

The outdoors is a neutral space and great equaliser. You don't know
if you are saying good morning to an executive, a politician, a truck
driver, a mature age student with a history of various jobs, a cleaner,
or an unemployed person who has never been taught their value and
abilities to contribute. You cannot see if they are illiterate or an English
literature teacher. It pays to be respectful to everyone. You don't ask
people what they do when they are in their swimwear. You tend to
interact on common ground, talking about the weather or the scenery.
You might say, "Is the weather always this gorgeous? Is this a typical
day here?" You are giving a little bit and then asking a bit back in
return with no sense of superiority or judgement.

It is okay if you are local and haven't met before or you are a visitor and
are being welcomed. Be open with the response you receive. Make it
okay for them to share something of themselves. If someone is shutting
down due to discomfort over a question, or looking suspicious or
defensive because of your question, you may have to give a little more
and say, "Oh I was just curious because …". Share why you are curious
and asked the question. There will be a reason why you asked, however
simple that is.

You may think you don't want to interrupt someone who looks like
they are having a great time, but if you are also enjoying the great
outdoors perhaps sharing the joy increases it for both of you. If you say
to someone "Isn't this a gorgeous day?" or "Aren't the clouds amazing?"
it is highly unlikely that they will respond negatively. It is far more likely
that they will be delighted to share it. My joy plus your joy could equal
so much more. There is an old Swedish quote that says, "A shared joy is
a double joy; shared sorrow is sorrow halved".

Workplaces

How many people line up to work in their ideal role, applying for one position after another, spending hours on proposals, applications – you know the paperwork, the research and the proofreading – preparing for the perfect interview. You think you're really in with a chance this time, you're perfect for the role, but it goes to someone who knew someone. The old "Better the devil you know" thinking. It's crazy isn't it – why settle for a devil they know, when you, an angel, are waiting in the wings? It's so true isn't it? It's not what you know, it's who you know.

So what can you do, to be the one 'who has it all'? You know the 'what', you have the experience, qualifications and, most importantly, the attitude and ability to learn and innovate, and the 'who'. Do you know the people who make the decisions or do you know someone who knows them? Have a think about the people you work with. Who do you pass in the lobby each day? Then consider who they might know. You would be familiar with some people in their network, but you only need to spend a few minutes on a social networking site (such as Facebook or LinkedIn) to see friends or connections who have mutual friends and so many more you don't know yet. Consider these people – who do they know? The possibilities are endless. What's next then? Raiding your friends or colleagues list and 'adding friends'? Perhaps not the best approach. I'm not recommending you do all your networking online either! Most of my connections around the world have come through face-to-face or phone meetings, actual conversations and genuine 'getting to know' each other.

Workplace conversations open up a new world of possibilities, but if you go looking for what you can get out of it, you may not be appreciated or tolerated by those you wish to connect with. A new connection might be worthwhile because a) you know or have something of value to share with the person you've met, or b) you know someone who has something that the person you've met needs or would appreciate. For example, if I can see how I can help Barry with something I have to give, or I can see that if I introduce him to Tash, she might be able to help him. Barry and I could help each other with a mutual support of some kind. I may not have anything Barry needs, but he might be happy to support me in some way. Why would he be interested in helping me? Because he's seen that I'm not just in it (the conversation, or the relationship) for what I can get out of it.

To quote Zig Ziglar – *"If you help enough people get what they want, you'll get everything you want"*.

So, while you need to be networking to build your opportunities, you also need to keep it genuine. Cut-throat competitiveness may work for a while, but you also want to sleep at night. I'm sure you want to arrive at your destination knowing that you are the right person for the job, confident in your relationships because you've built on a strong foundation of authenticity and generosity. Be the angel, not waiting in the wings, but stepping onto centre stage because of your connecting!

A friend told me a story of a man who hated going to work because his colleagues were "all bastards". He said, "No-one speaks to me. It is a horrible atmosphere". His wife suggested that he says good morning to them in a cheery voice as he goes in every morning. His response was, "I am not going to speak to them before they speak to me". If everyone in that office held that view, what a miserable place it would be.

I remember a customer at the bank I worked at who seemed determined to be grumpy every time she came in. The other staff told me that she was always like that and that I'd "never get a smile out of her" which only made me more determined. It took a week or two of expressing interest in her each day as she came in and flung her banking bag across the counter at me, but she warmed up. I think she really didn't like her job, but we connected on things like the beautiful day and anticipation of the weekend. So if you find yourself working alongside a grumpy person, don't take it personally, and find things to talk about that will put a smile on their face. I worked in sales with someone who rarely smiled, but when I asked after her daughter the smile would come.

Other friends have met the love of their life through their workplace. I recently met Brian East through AMP and he shared how he met his wife at a work social event and then saw each other around the office. Going to the blood bank together was a shared experience that connected them further. My friend Cate met her husband Clifford Stephens working at Target and loved waking up each day knowing she'd be working with her best friend all day. You never know who you'll meet and where your conversations will take you!

Pleasure before business

Tania's story: *In my second year of university, I was accepted to go to University of Alberta (UofA) in Edmonton, Canada as an exchange student during the second semester that year. I was thrilled. I am an avid scrapbooker and a loyal customer of direct selling business Creative Memories (CM). CM was founded in America and had consultants all over Canada. In April, almost five months before setting off on my adventure, I find a CM consultant near UofA and contact Carrie to see if it will be possible to buy some products while living in Edmonton as an exchange student. Carrie's email reply was warm and she tells me that her son Paul had been a student at the UofA and also had gone on exchange.*

In August, less than a month before my arrival in Edmonton, Carrie emails me wishing me a safe trip over and asks me to contact her once I'm settled – I do this and we arrange to meet for coffee. I remember standing outside my residency waiting for Carrie to pick me up and being so nervous. She takes me to her favourite café where she treats me to tea and cake and gives me a gift of some CM products that will be very useful in completing my exchange student adventure scrapbook. We talk and get to know each other. Carrie is a keen traveller and has been interested in visiting Australia. She was very warm and didn't even mention anything to me about buying products from her! By the time she dropped me home we had arranged another get together where she was going to take me to get my film developed and photos printed.

Over the months we saw each other in increasing frequency. At the time Paul was living and working overseas and she was missing him as I was missing my parents. By October we were calling each other replacement mom and replacement child. Towards the end of December Paul returned home and we finally got to meet. I was introduced – "Paul meet your sister Tania". Carrie has become my Canadian Mom (CM) and I her Aussie Daughter (AD).

A year after my return home Carrie flies to Australia for my 21st birthday and finally gets to fulfill her dream of visiting Australia. We had her stay with us and I spent two weeks showing her around Sydney and Melbourne. Two years later Carrie travels again to Australia for my wedding. Since then I've returned to Canada with my husband and we stayed with Carrie. It has now been 10 years since we met and we stay in regular contact.

I love Tania's story because of all the beautiful elements in it. This could easily have been a customer service experience that didn't disappoint or exceed expectations. It could have been just another business relationship. Carrie made a connection with her potential customer by sharing about her son, she took Tania out for coffee like an ambassador of her city, and was generous in spirit and in a practical way. She not only wins a friend, but eventually fulfills a dream of her own.

Connecting in an elevator without an 'elevator pitch'

Many people report silence and feeling uncomfortable when standing in a lift with strangers. A few of my friends have made great connections from brief encounters – and it hasn't been because they've been prepared with 'an elevator pitch' – a snappy, inspiring comment about what you do, designed to grab a prospective client's attention. No, they've simply been themselves, enthusiastic and in service of others.

Robyn McNeill was standing in an elevator when another woman stepped in. Robyn asked "what floor?" ready to press the button. They realized they were on their way to the same function. Not only did they both have someone to walk in with and sit with at the meeting, but Robyn soon employed her new friend as a media consultant who began raising Robyn's profile and her work was published in leading industry magazines. Her small act of kindness, a simple offer to press a button was an easy way to connect.

Anna Cochrane connected in a elevator one Friday night and received praise from her employers the next week when the following email arrived with the subject line: *Just met one of your amazing sales staff...*

> *Hi Xero*
>
> *Tonight, I checked into a hotel up here in Brisbane and when I got into the lift, I saw a lady wearing a Xero tshirt.*
>
> *As an avid user of the product, (world stores pty ltd), I said "omg you work for Xero... I love your product... Your payroll solution is cool".*
>
> *She had a good chuckle, and got out of the lift with me at my floor so we could keep talking.*

She introduced herself to me, and I now know that her name is Anna, and she moved to Aust from New Zealand a few years back.

Some feedback for you:

Firstly a great brand ambassador.... Wearing your tshirt at 9pm on a Friday night, and not afraid to have a great conversation about the product. You could tell she is genuinely excited about the company.

A very engaged employee. Working in HR, I was keen to understand what the culture was like at Xero. She spoke highly about the company and her experiences mirrored what you guys discuss on the website in terms of what it's like to work at Xero. Really good advocacy!!

In summary, if I wasn't already an existing user of the product, Anna's enthusiasm would have been enough to get me to at least consider looking into it. As I'm already a customer, what her enthusiasm has done is just cement my existing thinking about Xero, that is.... very cool cool company and very good product!

Please forward this email to Anna's boss. Keen for him or her to get this feedback

Josh Grace
Head of People and Culture at Foxtel

While Josh clearly was impressed with Anna's enthusiasm – I loved how he responded so generously and thoughtfully too. Anna's networking was not rehearsed but natural and authentic.

I met Linda from UCLA (University of California, Los Angeles) in the elevator in a hotel in San Francisco on the day before the 2011 Neuroleadership Summit. I stepped into the elevator to see colleagues from Australia and as I greeted them excitedly I also turned to the lady I thought was with them. With my hand out to greet her I said, "Hi I'm Kerrie - and you...?" She looked at me hesitantly so I continued, "you just happened to be in the lift?" Yes, she nodded. So that could have been an embarrassing moment but we laughed as we walked out of the elevator and fell into conversation about where we were headed. My colleagues left and Linda and I walked out the front door as she told me that she was also at the hotel for the Summit. She knew her way around the area and had a favourite Chinese restaurant nearby. We went there and had a wonderful meal and great conversations over the next couple of days.

While it's useful to define an "elevator pitch" for your own clarity, your brief opportunities for connection will be far more enjoyable and effective when you can be yourself, relaxed and interested in those nearby. That's when you're naturally confident and opportunities are more likely to flow.

Connection

The brain loves new things and when you are meeting a new person, if you let go of fear and inhibition, there are wonderful new discoveries. When you are making new discoveries your brain is forming connections at a faster pace, shifting to a more positive and creative way of seeing the world. When you are in a positive frame of mind you literally see more with your peripheral vision and your creative thinking expands.

A negative attitude causes you to be less alert and literally see less. Your peripheral vision is actually diminished. When you are downcast you literally look down, When you are looking up, you have an expanded view and your brain is more aware of what is going on around you and a sense of possibility that may be less tangible but still very real.

When I took my grandfather to Kokoda, PNG in 2012, we stayed in the village with a few other World War 2 veterans to commemorate the 70th commemoration of the Kokoda Campaign. Their stories, although from a very different situation, contained insights relevant to our everyday lives. Bede Tongs OAM MM (recipient of the Medal of the Order of Australia and the Military Medal) said "A positive attitude is essential for survival". I considered how relevant this is in the context of 'survival in business' or 'survival of relationships' and Bede shared evidence of this truth from his battle experiences. He made a comment one night "the miserable ones didn't last the distance" and explained how the negative, downcast soldiers were less observant, and more likely to be injured or killed.

Create a little toolkit for yourself for when you're feeling down. For example, little reminders, such as smiley-face stickers or a post-it-note on your computer screen. I have one that asks "Where is my focus now?" to help me get back on track. I might choose to wear something colourful to remind me of my focus during the day. It is okay to be deep in thought, and there are times when we need to be. But if you're feeling down it's quite likely that you're not present in the moment and you might trip up. Missing cues in a conversation is like not seeing a crack in the footpath.

COACHING CORNER

- What's in your toolbox for when you need a pick up?
- What else can you add to it?

Being present

Driving in Port Hedland, Western Australia, I was on a road that was parallel to the main road which has a higher speed limit. I was concentrating on where I was in relation to where I had to go. Not knowing the road, I was focused on the destination and checking that I was on the correct road. I was not focusing on my speed until the police sirens and lights went off. When the police told me I had been going 'a bit fast' I couldn't argue because I had no idea what speed I was going. I actually thanked the policeman because he'd just highlighted a great example of how the brain works. I think it may have been the only time the policeman had been thanked for giving out a speeding ticket. I really was not happy about paying a fine, but at least I could take a valuable insight to share with others.

Multi-tasking is actually switch-tasking; we switch our focus between several or multiple things. It is important to acknowledge that, since switch-tasking is actually less productive than focusing on one thing at a time. Of course we need to switch our attention to multiple things when we're driving to be aware of other cars, road conditions, gear changes needed and speed limits!

Focused attention is a more an intense thinking space than being present. Focused attention is a bit like being in a tunnel – hence the term 'tunnel vision'. You are concentrating on one element and have actually tuned out to the rest of the environment around you. You focus attention in the morning on the train to get to work. You might focus on your electronic device rather than the station where you'll be getting off. You may not remember any of the hundreds of people on the train with you. If however you are being present you will be amazed at all the interesting people at the train station, on the train, and on your walk to work. It makes your brain lighter.

It is often little things that we get excited about, but they put a smile on your face. We have a strong sense of connection not only to people, but to places. We have a whole set of mental maps that are energising to revisit. We make a connection with an existing map and add more detail. In some ways we seem more connected to those around us in the world, but the depth of our connection can be shallow.

We are bombarded with invitations and opportunities through social media, or email or mass mail-out, but when we get a personal invitation like a hand-written invitation or phone call there is a greater sense of connection and we feel special because someone has taken the time to connect. We want to feel special, connected and appreciated. We don't want to feel like we are just another number to fill a room.

RIGHT ATTITUDE

The following stories are examples of attitudes that open doors of connection and opportunity. You'll have your own language for this, and in different scenarios a different attitude will be the 'right attitude'. For example, it could be an attitude of curiosity, openness, positivity, joy or empathy. As you read these stories, remember the moments you've found yourself in the sweet spot of the right place, the right person, with the right attitude. We have a common saying "right place, right time" and these stories are examples of this, with a deeper look into what's going on in these serendipitous moments.

Choosing to be open

I was catching a train to the Central Coast to see my friend Olivia Lockwood, who had travelled from the USA. I found a small carriage where there were only three rows of seats. Two rows were facing each other creating a pod where I had four seats to myself. So being the most spacious area, with my entire luggage I moved into that row. The train wasn't very busy so I thought I might have the space to myself. I was quite looking forward to having the time to think and write. Just before the train left the station a tall African man walked through the carriage looking for a seat and paused on seeing luggage blocking him from sitting in those seats. He hesitated and I said I was happy to share the space. I just wasn't sure where to put my suitcase. He put his textbook down on the seat beside me and lifted my suitcase onto the opposite seat facing me.

I noticed Martin Luther King Jr. (and President Obama) on the cover of the textbook and said, "It's 50 years today since his 'I Have A Dream' speech!", which mum had mentioned to me earlier that morning on the plane. He lit up and said yes enthusiastically and then sat down beside me. Normally I think he would have sat diagonally opposite and I think that was his original plan. Because I had engaged him he sat next me. If it had been a busy train, it would have been normal to sit next to me, but because it was quiet it was momentarily uncomfortable. We unconsciously create a concept of a proper amount of space in relation to the environment. He sat down beside me in his enthusiasm and I was aware of the tendency to draw back. I opted to offer him some of the biscuits I had just opened and he said yes thank you as he reached into the packet. He placed his other hand on my wrist and rubbed it gently and said almost in amazement, "How are you so friendly?" I was lost for words and paused.

I think because of his surprise at my friendliness, I was surprised also and wondered if he had not experienced simple kindness very often. It made me glad I had been kind and I chose to be open towards him. I saw that it was a conscious choice because I was aware that there were other passengers opposite us and wondered what it looked like from the outside. I began to question myself as to whether I would be judged by other people. I am sitting quite close, should he be leaning this close? Nothing is going to happen to me with other people on the train. There were a number of thoughts rushing through my mind and awareness of my thinking and my surroundings all at once.

It was a moment of choosing to trust, and to let go of expectations of others or my perception of society's norms. In normal rational thought we would say it doesn't matter what total strangers think. We do hold back from connecting to someone because of what the surrounding strangers may think about us. We think the judgement of total strangers doesn't affect us, but it does inhibit us. On the surface you might read and think that the judgement of others does not affect us, but dig a little deeper and you realise that we do change our behaviour for societal acceptance. In being really honest you are open to judging from others who are not being honest with themselves. Even writing this requires that I open up to being vulnerable, in a position to be judged by you, the reader.

The reader is also willing to be vulnerable as well. And hopefully you are not reading this in a rush so you can feel the vulnerability. Take the time to think of when you have stopped talking when others get into an elevator or wanted to talk to someone on the other side of the train but have been aware of the other people on the train. Is that honestly not wanting to disturb the other passengers or is it a fear of judgement or misunderstanding? The "I don't want to disturb anyone" can be an excuse for not being brave enough to speak up. We do not want to draw attention to ourselves.

He offered his hand and said, "My name is Jerome". Although I have heard the name I have not known another Jerome. So I said, "It is a lovely name, do you know what it means?" He said, "No, but Jerome was the translator of the bible into Latin from the original text". An amazing 75-minute conversation unfolded as he shared about his life growing up in the Democratic Republic of Congo, including 15 years in a refugee camp. He called it the DRC – the "Dangerous Republic of Congo". He shared that he helped in Rwanda after the genocide and he was very excited that I had been mentoring a young Rwandan man. Jerome had been finding families to take in the orphaned children after the genocide.

Jerome offered to keep in touch and wrote down his email and the following message, "A friendship is like a seed. It needs to be sowed, germinated watered, grow up and then provide both shade and fruits. Our seed of friendship is sowed today, grows up and bears fruit". He told me about his mother in Africa who sounds amazing. I felt richer for the experience. I learned that she "only walks about 20 kilometres" now to deliver babies as she is 80 years old. The women come to her now, rather than her walking exceedingly long distances to deliver. I learned about his family and those most precious to him as he spoke from his heart, delighted to share his story.

I was aware of others in the train noticing our conversation, how Jerome touched my arm a few times. I wondered what they were thinking, seeing that I let a stranger touch me. I chose to overcome the tendency to draw back and create more space between us. I was aware of thinking I 'should', but I asked myself if I really needed to. If he's being warm, genuine and innocent, who is to deem it inappropriate, especially if it encourages him to be acknowledged and listened to? Who can judge his motives, and who can judge how I should respond in that moment? I told him about my husband and son. He told me about his wife and he was beaming just thinking of her. This increased the sense of safety and the intuitive sense that I could remain 'in' this conversation.

He told me about how his wife had managed to escape the Gatumba massacre in Burundi in 2004. I asked him how she managed that and he looked me in the eyes and paused as if asking if it was safe to share, if his story would be believed… "It was a miracle", he said. Jerome and his wife had been in separate refugee camps and didn't see each other for about 10 years. Her name is Immaculée. He asked did I know what that meant and I said "Is it like immaculate, pure?" He said "Yes, without spot or blemish." He wrote down key names, places and events for me to search online. He gave me links to articles in the Newcastle Herald and Hunter Woman Newcastle.

I felt the conversation was a privilege and that talking with Jerome expanded my worldview. My eyes are welling up as I retell this story now. It's just so far removed from our everyday Australian culture. He had lived through hell for so many years in his life and helped pick up the pieces in Rwanda since the 1994 genocide. I felt in awe of his beautiful attitude and happy disposition in the face of his experiences.

He showed no signs of bitterness. It was a joy to discuss the ways in which these war torn places are being helped, and I was able to share with him about my friend Trishelle Grady who is building an orphanage and school in Uganda.

I was so pleased that I had decided to be open to this conversation. I could have missed this incredible story, which I felt grew me as a person. In the beginning I was on the phone to my Lyndon so perhaps I could have chosen to just keep talking and ignore him completely. People might think I'm just a chatterbox who talks to everyone and starts the conversation, but sometimes these conversations come to me, as long as I am open to the possibility and I choose to be curious.

In business we are encouraged to tell stories and work on our elevator pitch and talk about what we do, but there is not so much emphasis on listening. When we really listen to people we develop our curiosity and we grow so much more. It is very easy to be self-absorbed, but when you decide to show an interest in others you'll find that their lives are fascinating and you can learn as much – or more –than you can ever teach. This was just the start of a 'being open' weekend. Great things in life often happen on the way to doing the things that you have planned. It is not necessarily in the things that we plan, the big events. And that is why it is so important to practice being present, in the moment.

I had a wonderful 24 hours on the Central Coast of New South Wales with Olivia before I boarded another train where another surprising encounter occurred on my way back to Central Station in Sydney. I was alone in the carriage until the next station on the coast. I was in the section where the disabled and elderly seats are located. It is easier when I am travelling with luggage not to lug it up and down train stairs. A lady hopped on with two young boys. With my back to the window, she was on the same side as me about a metre down, and one boy sat opposite her. The other boy decided to hang off the handles, swinging back and forth, like I would have done if I were his age.

Just before the train left the station a slender woman in a gorgeous dress raced in and sat opposite me and then said, "Is this train definitely going to Central?" in a slightly anxious voice. "This is definitely the train to Sydney", I said. "I just double-checked that myself". The other lady said yes at the same time and the two ladies recognised each other. They were straight into conversation. I had missed the opportunity to compliment her on her dress, so I left them to talk and turned back to my emails on my phone. Ten minutes later the lady opposite caught my eye and said, "Do you two know each other?" I said, "No, because if I did I would have been in your conversation – although I tried not to eavesdrop - it sounded interesting". They had been talking about online and creative businesses. The three of us chatted for the next hour and Shayne (the lady sitting opposite me) invited us both to hear her daughter sing. Her 19-year-old daughter was performing her songs that night in Sydney.

When the lady next to me left the train with her boys, Shayne moved over to the same side of the carriage as me and we continued chatting. As we left Central Station, I still hadn't heard from my friend Natalie who I'd planned to meet up with later so I decided to walk down to China Town. Shayne was going that way too, so we walked together. She said, "I haven't done this since I was a teenager; you know meeting someone and saying let's hang out together". It was fun. I decided that her comment had to go into this book so I made a note of it in my phone immediately. I loved the sense of fun with which she said it. We discussed how as adults we get so serious and busy and we need to be more open to fun, spontaneous moments and connections. I have heard it said that it is harder to make new friends when we are older. We seem to have shut down our curiosity and openness to others. We've lost our innocence and faith in people somehow.

Shayne and I continued discussing how connecting with strangers is a two-way street. We had both stepped into the unknown at different moments of the conversation and taken the conversation and experience further. We'd only just met, so either of us could pull back and say "you go ahead" – possibly thinking 'I didn't mean I wanted to hang out with you'. It is the next little step that takes the relationship further, taking you in either of two directions. It may end the conversation or further the relationship.

We exchanged phone numbers and parted ways, assuming we would make contact again, but knowing that there were no strings attached if either of us didn't want to pursue the connection further. We both felt we could have chatted longer, but Shayne needed to meet up with her friend and I needed to get to the shops before they closed. I helped her find directions to the hotel where she was meeting someone using my phone maps. Later in the afternoon I received a text message, "We're at the dumpling café". Taking it as an invitation I responded with, "Is there room for an extra?" I still had some time up my sleeve so I called and Shayne gave me directions. I walked around to the dumpling café where she introduced me to her friend. We shared how we met and the three of us had a great conversation over dumplings and green tea. When her partner arrived I was introduced like an old friend. Assuming this, he asked if I was a school friend. I said, "We go way back, oh about an hour".

It was lovely to feel welcomed into her circle of friends and community. Sometimes it is the spontaneous friendships that are not taking the customary path that give us more joy because they are just that – spontaneous and unexpected. We discovered more and more things to talk about and shared interests and shared connections. If these became less and less the friendship dies a natural death and that is okay. In both cases we have connected on Facebook because of those shared interests and mutually beneficial contacts.

Shayne was open to walk with me to China Town and took a risk inviting me to dinner. What if her friends didn't like me? She trusted that my presence wouldn't be intrusive into her group's experience. How many times in a day do we have opportunities to be open and trust in others? As I was writing this chapter, I sent a text thanking Shayne for these insights and connection and she soon texted back:

> That's very cool. Thanks! Yes, I agree totally: I talk to dogs, little old ladies, teens or housewives, i don't discriminate, lol (actually, i do tend to avoid Suits, my only prejudice)! I say we all need to get our heads out of our a**es and iphones and start engaging! You never know when u might stumble across a kindred spirit :-)
> Shayne xox

This concept of 'being open' revisited me in the next 24 hours through my next new friend who I met later that same night. After leaving Shayne and her friends and thanking them for their company, I found the hotel that Natalie had booked. She and I went shopping for snacks. It was getting late and I was tired and ready to leave. I walked back down an aisle to where Natalie was still making a decision, and as I waited for her a tall lady in a stunning purple jacket walked up the aisle. I caught her eye and said, "What a great jacket". Her face lit up and she said thank you and shared that she was a bit warm but she had needed it in Melbourne where she had just come from.

We chatted for about five or 10 minutes starting with our shared appreciation for colour, her jacket and her comfortable and gorgeous purple Israeli shoes. She mentioned she was in town for a trade show. I thought she might know friends of mine from Melbourne in the same industry and I gave her my card just in case she ran into them tomorrow. We discovered that the trade show Yvette was attending was in Darling Harbour, not far from the event we were going to. We said goodbye and wished each other a great weekend.

The next day when Natalie and I arrived at the conference centre for "The Unconvention", I noticed a sign listing the trade show at the other end of the same building and realised I had left her business card in my hotel room. I couldn't text her to "have a great day" as I would have if I'd had the card. Towards the end of the day, I was on my own at the back of the conference hall and my phone rang with a number I didn't recognise and it was Yvette, who I had met the night before. She had rung to see if I was nearby and realised only two floors separated us when she could see me below in the foyer. I invited her down and she joined me for the end of the Unconvention and VIP event afterwards.

Yvette told us later that night, "I was wondering what to do as I had no takers for dinner and thought I will go back to my hotel room… I'd rather hang out with a friend… I'll ring Kerrie". This is a woman I had spoken to at the supermarket for five minutes. But when she was looking for a friend in town she thought of me. That totally made my day.

Friendship in this case was a sense of connection even though we hadn't known each other long. She had a sense that it was okay to call about whether I was free to meet up or not. So we went for dinner after the VIP event. After dinner, which Natalie joined us for, we went for dessert and we talked about, among many things, talking to strangers and connecting to people. Yvette talked about how she had decided to call me and be open to people because of a lovely encounter that had impacted her life overseas many years ago with a stranger who'd become a friend. We talked about how we can close ourselves off and it diminishes the opportunities to making beautiful connections.

All three of these stories were wonderful unexpected encounters that happened because of the 'in the moment' choices Jerome, Shayne, Yvette and I had made, choices to be open, curious and accepting. They were not the reason I had gone to Sydney. I went to enjoy time with Olivia and attend a conference where I knew I would have great moments of connection. It was the surprising encounters beyond the planned schedule that gave me unexpected joy. That is why it is great to be open in everyday life, not just go out to events or schedule activities with your networking face on. Just be yourself and be open to connecting and encouraging others.

If you go out with your networking face on and ready to deliver your elevator pitch over and over, regardless of how well you deliver your story, you will not engage the same way as when you are genuinely interested in others. Yvette had sensed that I was genuinely interested in her story in the supermarket aisle. I wasn't seeing her as a prospective client, referral source or with any other agenda. We can just connect for the joy of it. She was encouraged by a simple comment about her jacket. We all love a compliment, especially about our favourite things/clothes/people. Let's look for opportunities to compliment others and accept compliments when they're given to us. Yvette saw me without judgement and assumed the best, that it was me just saying what I thought, no strings attached.

I have a policy that if you think something positive and if there is an opportunity to share it – go for it. We need more positivity in the world. Some people think something negative and think it has to be said.

The Book of Proverbs says – *"The tongue has the power of life and death, and those who love it will eat its fruit".*

Your words will affect you. Your words also affect others. You've felt it. Your words are powerful and can have an effect that is greater than you realise. Just when you think you are having a bad hair day or you need a little encouragement, someone might say, "Your hair looks great today" or "That colour is great on you". You walk away relieved and uplifted. They've seen something positive that you haven't and it's a wonderful perspective shifter.

Have you ever noticed that your general sense of confidence can be shifted up or down by the quality of your hair cut or style or the colour you wear? We don't have a complete view of ourselves and can be quite hard on ourselves. If someone can share some positive feedback it can be very useful. How can you offer that to others?

You need to have a safe trusting relationship to say that jacket doesn't suit you as much as your other one, but we can all offer something positive and expect that it will generally be appreciated. It is like offering a small gift. It is okay if the would-be recipient doesn't receive it – that is their choice. A song from my childhood comes to mind – "This little light of mine, I'm going to let it shine".

Choosing Joy

Let your joy, your vibrancy, and your love of life shine through. It is so easily contained, but if you let it out you will find it is good for you and good for others. If your joy, vibrancy or enthusiasm is waning, there is hope. We all have times when our joy, vibrancy and enthusiasm are a little lacking. At other times, it is hard to see how you could ever be vibrant again. I know life is full of challenges. But it's also full of joys. Uplifting moments, the bounce in the step, the feeling of gratitude, even if things aren't going well. It's not a circumstantial thing, it's a focus thing. It's great to ask yourself – where is my focus right now? Look beyond the obvious. Clearly, you're focusing on the words on the page, but what are you really focused on?

Joy is available to us everyday – but it doesn't come looking for us. We need to look for it and generate it. It's SO possible, even in a crazy busy world, to discover joy in the everyday. I remember the first time I saw Jamie Oliver on TV, throwing together a salad, passionately discussing the ingredients. He made this comment: "Fresh mint in a salad is just a joy", and I thought, 'Oh Jamie, you're just a joy'. I became a fan immediately. I was inspired by his way of seeing the world and I love that his work is what he absolutely delights in. That doesn't mean that everything in his life is fabulous; he has challenges just like everyone else. We all do, but we can find what we are passionate about and we can discover joys that aren't always obvious.

So this is an invitation to go discover the joy in your every day. What are the little things that light you up? Maybe it's the trees or the clouds or the brilliant blue of the sky. Maybe it's the smell of coffee or strawberries. Yum! You could miss them so easily, but they're all around us. There are many things in the everyday that you can find joy in. And one of the best ways to change your state or perspective in order to find the joy is noticing things you can be grateful for.

It's okay if it's just a choice at the moment and you don't feel joyful but you choose to notice it and put pen to paper. List (or draw) what you are grateful for, like living somewhere that has air conditioning, being grateful for a roof over your head. Really – imagine if you didn't! You will start to find more and more things to be grateful for and you will start to see more of those things appearing in your life.

As I was getting ready for a 7am breakfast, I posted a good morning kind of comment on Facebook. It was quite early and I had a giggle to myself as I imagined that some people might see it and say, "Ugh! Not another morning person!" I wanted to go back and add, "I'm not a morning person!" It can take me a while to get going, but if I need to I won't get out of bed until I've written at least one thing (usually three things) that I'm grateful for and I CHOOSE to get up and have a great day. Playing an uplifting song is the next thing I do. I need help and reminders to choose my focus many times. And I discover joy in everyday life.

A recent favourite is *Speak Life* by Toby Mac. It's a great reminder of the power of words. One of the songs I've had on my phone for years which never ceases to lose it's joy is *Rainy Day* by Kate Spence-Wray – here's a few lines that paint a beautiful picture.

> *"I wake up in a brand new day, I've never lived this day before,*
> *God help me not to be wasteful of this gift of time.*
> *I've been given a chance at life, oh how good it is to be alive,*
> *My mission today is make the world a brighter place"*
> *Put a smile on everyone's face*
>
> *Oh life can be such joy, I want the world to experience it.*
> *Even on a rainy day the sun still lives above the clouds,*
> *even if you're feeling sad laughter will soon come out,*
> *I'm going to make the most of today, I'll never live it, see it,*
> *breathe it again".*

How can you generate joy, or find joy, in the little things today? My family and I were driving home from Bathurst and we bought some lollies and fruit for the way home. The lollies were 'disguises' like lemon-flavoured moustaches, teeth lollies, berry-flavoured red lips and lime-green eyebrows. Following Ethan's lead, we pressed the lollies to our lips, teeth, upper lip and eyebrows, giggling about how silly we looked. The phone came out and we took photos and had many laughs trying to get them to stick while we got all our faces together for the photo. To be honest, when Ethan wanted me to post a photo on Facebook, I felt that it was too silly and not professional.

A year later, Ethan was doing an assignment for his Chinese class about family. He printed one of those photos and shared it in his assignment as a favourite moment. He chose it as a favourite family memory, a moment that was inexpensive, silly, funny and connecting. In our adult world of being busy, professional and preoccupied with the opinions of others, we steal our own joy and that of others – often those most important to us.

When I considered what my most recent favourite family moment was, it was the family photo shoot that we did on the trampoline. The three of us jumped as high as we could while our photographer clicked away. Sometimes we held hands and all the time we laughed at the challenges of jumping at the same time. The photos show moments of hysterical laughter, chaos as limbs went where they weren't meant to. Sometimes one of us was flat on our back or we were falling all over ourselves.

A fun photo shoot was my idea and a decision to push against the natural tendency to sit down and smile graciously for a portrait. Moments of silliness sometimes need to be deliberately chosen and life does give us those opportunities. If we spill something we can get serious or we can see the funny side of life. Children are free and having fun – free to be silly. Adults often say "Don't be silly" in an attempt to discipline children, not knowing that they are training the joy out of the moment and their later life. Have you ever challenged yourself, that when given an opportunity to look silly, to go with it?

I met Michael because he was looking silly. He was standing outside a store in Perth Hay Street Mall selling the *Big Issue* magazine. I saw him across the street because he had pink rabbit ears with flashing lights on his head and a little Dalmatian puppy nose on his face. I walked into the store when he was speaking to some people and watched their faces through the window. I stood and watched for a while as he connected or didn't connect with people as they passed by.

Some tried not to look at him, some people smiled or smirked to themselves and looked away. Others smiled at him and acknowledged him as they walked by and others stopped, chatted and bought the magazine. I think some bought it without much conversation and I wondered what their perspective of him was. Did they just buy it because they felt sorry for him? Did they buy it to do their good deed for the day, or because they like the articles? It's so easy to interact with someone in a sales situation without giving them a second glance. I pondered awhile and thought I had better get back to my friend's office so I left the store to head back.

As I walked across the street I felt I was walking away from an opportunity. I didn't know what that opportunity would be but I was curious. I turned and stood watching again and as people walked away from him and standing alone, he saw me looking at him smiling. He called out "What are you laughing at?" with a smile on his face. I walked towards him and said, "I am not laughing, I am smiling, and fascinated about how you connect with people". I told him I was interested in how strangers connect because I was writing a book about it and enjoy connecting with people myself. Obviously one of his keys to connecting is by being a little quirky and wearing various headpieces. It gets their attention because not every day do you see a grown man wearing something silly. You can't help but notice and choose to smile or look away, depending on your judgements.

Michael told me that people like to have a chat. "Sometimes people just like to have someone to talk to. I have people come and talk to me and cry on my shoulder." With his friendly face, easy disposition and open expression I wasn't surprised. He told me a little about his history. He was very well spoken and well educated as he told me about the private schools he attended in India and London. When he moved to Australia he worked in various roles that involved talking to people including door knocking for real estate sales.

As we were talking a young couple walked past and I heard a negative, tone of voice saying "Big Issue". I asked Michael what was that about. He replied, "Some people are just a bit mean. Sometimes they are rude and sometimes they say why don't you get a real job? I am in my 70s, what else am I going to do?" We spoke for about half an hour and as he packed up his gear, he told me he was going to the theatre that night. We asked a man nearby to take a photo of us together sitting on the park bench. As I left him I walked through to the mall with a huge smile on my face. That would have made people wonder what I was up to. I had a skip in my step and I couldn't wait to tell my friends who I had met. Michael's silliness opened doors, made my day (generated joy), and I think it made his day to sit and chat with me too. Sharing his story in this book might also have an impact.

The way to generate joy is usually with the little things. We tend to over complicate things and joy is in the simplicity of the world around us. We think we need a big fix and put happiness on hold waiting for the big change. My first full-time job in a dental surgery was a very fast-paced role with a lot of pressure to keep everything spotless and sterile, while looking after people and keeping them at ease. I'm glad the team I worked with were fun, and moments of silliness kept us going. I surprised Annette in the office sometimes by serving her tea with a jelly snake wrapped around the cup handle – and when I saw her in hospital a few years later I gave her a card with a red snake included which made her laugh. Which is not a good thing to do to someone who's recently had surgery…

Joy can be found in new perspectives. It might be:

- walking slower and observing the world
- looking for things that make you smile
- sitting in a café and looking for the happiest faces walking by
- watching children laugh

- watching the sunrise or sunset
- getting out in nature
- closing down technology to enjoy the view or have a conversation
- water
- skipping
- smiling
- watching the joy of dogs running on the beach
- happy music
- happy faces
- good food that doesn't have guilt attached
- being silly
- exercise
- writing
- getting enough sleep.

Why am I so friendly?

When Jerome asked this of me on the train, the question bounced around in my mind, the echo of his intrigue apparent as he waited, completely present. I searched for the answer to why I am so friendly. Even as I share this story with friends now, the question is always the same … "So what did you say?" What did I say? I know I was lost for words, and how do I articulate – how is it that I am so friendly?

How do I answer that? Is it my innate nature? Is it my upbringing with friendly people, parents who know that people matter? Is it the DNA of my parents, or the DNA of Jesus Christ, the ultimate connector? Is it because I was bullied and left out throughout my school years that has tuned me in to people who are alone or lacking confidence and the knowledge that someone cares? Is it that I've learned from experience that it really makes a significant difference to someone's life, or just their day? It really can be the difference between success and failure, between life and death. Is it growing up with *Choose Your Own Adventure* books and seeing that every decision you make has consequences?

It's essentially a choice to connect with others. One of my friends tells me it's her choice to let her husband be the connector. In our conversations about this book, she's realised what she was missing out on. She recalls, "You got me connecting with people and I would never have had the opportunity to meet some of the people I've met now."

I picked up my mum from a shopping centre recently and she was so excited about the connection she'd just made with a lady in the food court. She said, "I have just had this amazing conversation with this lady who will be 90 in five weeks' time – she was a prisoner of war in Germany. She grew up in Ukraine and went to a Russian school and came to Australia in 1949, and she speaks seven languages and is a language teacher. What got me chatting with her was her colourful outfit and scarves that were knitted".

When Mum first saw her she said, "Oh hello! You look lovely... did you make these?" And the lady replied, "No I am a language teacher". Mum was sorry that she had to leave her as she felt that they could've talked for ages. So many people share these kinds of stories with me – the simple joy of discovering someone who has an interesting story.

My friend Maria in Italy says, "I will never stop connecting with people. I still have several millions to meet!!" So my challenge to you is to go out and DO talk to strangers – connect with anyone, anywhere – and please write and tell me your stories!

FINAL THOUGHTS

I have realised as I complete this book that this book will never really be complete. There will always be more stories and insights I could have shared – some make it to my blog, and some to my public presentations. Some are shared in conversations over coffee, and some are simply cherished in the moment.

Many readers have great stories and insight everyday, which are often shared in our Do Talk To Strangers group on Facebook. Special thanks go out to all of these inspiring connectors and contributors.

There will always be names of people I wish I'd included - I do hope you know that I appreciate you reading this far and that you do matter. You are important and valued. So many people make up my world and I am so grateful for each one of you.

You can make an enormous difference in the lives of others as you realize your value and your influence and use it wisely. I really hope that above all, you've seen this as you've shared these pages with me.

In the ASKING Model, under "Interest in Others" I shared a quote by St Francis of Assisi. It comes from the following prayer, which I carried around in a wallet for years when I was a school girl. I can't think of a better note to finish on.

> *Lord, make me an instrument of Your peace. Where there is hatred, let me sow love; where there is injury, pardon; where there is doubt, faith; where there is despair, hope; where there is darkness, light; where there is sadness, joy.*
>
> *O, Divine Master, grant that I may not so much seek to be consoled as to console; to be understood as to understand; to be loved as to love. For it is in*

giving that we receive; it is in pardoning that we are pardoned; it is in dying that we are born again to eternal life.

- St Francis of Assisi

PART THREE

Resources, gratitude
and connecting
with the author

RECOMMENDED RESOURCES

Videos

My favourite TED Talks include Brene Brown on 'The Power of Vulnerability' and 'Listening To Shame' and Simon Sinek on 'How Great Leaders Inspire Action', and 'Why Good Leaders Make You Feel Safe'.

See www.TED.com for an incredible supply of inspiring, insightful resources. Amanda Palmer and Amy Cuddy have also presented some of my favourite TED Talks. I recommend spending some time browsing this amazing library for short videos, no longer than 20 minutes and packed full of insightful research and ideas.

My video channel is often updated with brief conversations about connecting, and interviews with insightful, creative people. Access via www.kerriephipps.com or YouTube.

Books

My library is enormous and I love to share its contents. Here are a few that have added to my learning over recent years. If you have a chance to hear any of these authors speak, do what it takes to get there.

- *You Are Not Your Brain*
  Jeffrey Schwartz, M.D. and Rebecca Gladding, M.D.
- *Mindsight – The New Science Of Personal Transformation*
  Daniel J. Siegel, M.D.
- *Social: Why Our Brains Are Wired to Connect*
  Matt Lieberman
- *Mindset: The New Pyschology of Success*
  Carol S. Dweck, Ph.D

- *Your Brain At Work*
  David Rock
- *Everyone Communicates, Few Connect*
  John Maxwell
- *Bounce Forward - How to Transform Crisis into Success*
  Sam Cawthorn
- *Wired For Life – Retrain Your Brain and Thrive*
  Susan Pearse and Martina Sheehan
- *As A Man Thinketh*
  James Allen
- *The Holy Bible* - Popular translations include *New Living Translation*, *New King James Version*, and *The Message*.

Other books by Kerrie

 *Create the Life Journal: Write Your Way To The Life You Want*

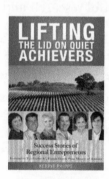 *Lifting The Lid on Quiet Achievers: Success Stories of Regional Entrepreneurs*

Kerrie Phipps is a contributing author in the following books:

- *Create Your Dream Sanctuary*
  Victoria Millar-Wise, 2009
- *Live Your Passion – People & Performance*
  Michael & Jane Pelusey, 2011
- *I Am Woman*
  Minda Lennon 2011
- *Customer Service*
  Kizzy Nkwocha 2012
- *The Solo Traveller's Compass*
  Justine Waddington 2014

MY GRATITUDE

Many thanks to all who have taught me more about how the brain works - Dr Jessica Payne, Dr Matt Leiberman, Dr David Rock, Dr Daniel Siegel, Dr Ray Andrews and Georgia Lush. And my coaches, colleagues, mentors and clients over many years – you inspire, encourage and empower me.

Jane Pelusey – thank you for connecting with me, for typing as I rambled on with many stories, for sharing your smoothies, your long beach walks and favourite cafes along Perth's coastline. Thanks Michael for not only letting us talk all day, but bringing us cups of tea to keep us going! Thank you both for stepping out of the comfort zone with me at my events and joining me on a high ropes course adventure.

Nathan Shooter – you inspire me more than you know. Thank you for bringing your spirit of excellence to all the work we do.

Sam Cawthorn – thanks for trusting this stranger to drive you home, and for all the inspiring conversations and connections since. Your visionary gifting is extraordinary and I'm so grateful for you and your team.

Kylie Henderson – angel of creativity and encouragement, thanks for the extra editing, and for turning up when most needed.

Louise D'Allura – you are a GEM my friend. So grateful for your friendship and ever fresh perspective and expertise.

David Hooper – it is incredible what has unfolded since we met at the Western Australian book launch of Lifting The Lid on Quiet Achievers with James and Penny Taylor. Thank you for welcoming me to speak at C3 Port Hedland over the past few years and connecting me with your wonderful community. Thanks for sharing your drawings, insights and encouragement.

Mum and Dad – the world is an extraordinary place, but there's no place like home, no family like our family. I love you so much and I'm so grateful for your incredible support.

Lyndon and Ethan – my darling champions. Thank you for sharing the journey, thanks for the love and the good food, Lyndon for office management, and Ethan, transcribing my conversations with Jane. What a team! To the journey.

The Cafés I sat and wrote in, the customers and staff who shared their stories, Taxi drivers and fellow commuters on buses, trains and planes – thanks for all the conversations, the laughs and the insights.

To every reader… thank you for sharing these pages with me. Keep growing, learning and connecting. You make a bigger difference than you know.

THE IMPACT OF YOUR CONTRIBUTION

It's highly likely that you make a greater contribution to the world around you than you realise. To raise awareness of how we can make a bigger difference in the world, it's important to be aware of how you naturally contribute already. We're aware of so much hurt and pain in our world and can be overwhelmed by it, so we must remember that each individual makes a difference and it matters that you add your voice, your talents and gifts to contribute to others.

Even by purchasing this book, or receiving it as a gift, more gifts have been given. For every book purchased, life-giving water has been provided to families in developing nations.
Every time I connect with an audience to inspire more connections and ideas, students and entrepreneurs receive quality mentoring and education.

We do this through B1G1 (www.b1g1.com), Kokoda Track Foundation (www.kokodatrackfoundation.org) and several other trusted organisations. We don't wait until we have a lot to give; we give a specific percentage of whatever funds land in our account.
My son and I discovered first hand in Cambodia how one dollar can make a difference, and when there are many people contributing in the ways they do best, significant change occurs.

Consider how you contribute to the world around you, with your smiles, your encouragement, your funds and your time. You make a difference, keep up the great work!

Kerrie

www.kerriephipps.com

ABOUT THE CONTRIBUTORS

Jane Pelusey

Known for authoring over 80 books and hundreds of magazine articles, Jane Pelusey loves bringing stories to life. The Pelusey's books are published by Macmillan, Hema Maps and through their independent publishing business Pelusey Publishing. Their articles and photographs have been published in magazines such as Australian Geographic, Club Marine, RM Williams Outback, 4WD Action and Caravan and Motorhome magazines and many newspapers.

Jane helps others to tell their story through book mentorships and speaking internationally on books and publishing. She is passionate about tapping into people's talents and knowledge so they can share their story.

Jane Pelusey and her photographer husband, Michael, are also professional travellers who write and capture scenes to encourage others to explore the world. Their knowledge of travel and the travel mindset has resulted in many publications and speaking engagements.

www.pelusey.com
jane@pelusey.com

David Hooper

David and Lil Hooper have lived in Port Hedland for over 24 years, where their three children were born and raised. David is a local Artist, Pastor and Town of Port Hedland Councillor. They enjoy the outdoor life of the Pilbara, including BBQ's and 4x4 on the beach and love the town and it's people.

"I've been in Port Hedland since following my girlfriend Lil's parents up here in 1989. We all came from Whangarei in New Zealand. NZ is hilly and green, whereas here it is flat and red, so it's almost as contrasting as Earth and Mars. But I love this Rusty Country!

Throughout my life, art and painting have remained a constant, and I dedicate one day per week to doing artwork. Something I've noticed about myself is that when I'm looking at an artwork, I love to see simplicity: simplicity but effectiveness. Anything worth watching in art – whether it's a gymnast, or a diver, or something of beauty – they make it look so easy and yet it's only because they're putting in all the effort beforehand; and so I like to see that in art... and take you to a happy place.

I serve as Pastor at C3, where our church exists to serve the community. C3 currently has over 300 churches around the world and our tagline is, Your Best Life.

I also serve on the local Town of Port Hedland Council; I'm in my second four-year term. This has been a challenging but rewarding journey. We are a growing town/city, and there's a lot of work and leadership to be done!"

www.hoop.gallery
david.hooper@me.com

ABOUT THE AUTHOR

Kerrie Phipps began her great life adventure in 1973 on a farm near Gilgandra NSW, where work and play were often simultaneous. Kerrie has always been passionate about serving people, so employment in dental nursing, banking and sales gave her many opportunities to encourage and connect.

Passionate about making a bigger difference everyday, Kerrie dedicated 8 years to serving young people and youth leaders by providing small to large-scale youth events in the western region of NSW along with many hours of one-to-one mentoring, hospitality and leadership development.

A chronic illness put a stop to this lifestyle and opened the door to profound breakthroughs in her thinking as she learned to face new challenges with a focus on solutions and setting achievable goals. It was 2004 when Kerrie discovered personal/business coaching as the perfect fit for her passion to serve and empower people. She took on a coach to support her full recovery, designing a new lifestyle and creating a difference-making business.

Her coach was regional-based Georgia Lush, Global Head of Training for Results Coaching Systems. Excited by the idea that one could run a business from home, and with a love of learning Kerrie threw herself into extensive training with RCS, now known as The Neuroleadership Group.

Kerrie earned the Results Certified Coach credential, and represented The Neuroleadership Group globally as a consultant and mentor for hundreds of coaches and built her own business coaching entrepreneurs and leaders.

As a Keynote Speaker and Conference Culture Specialist, Kerrie excels in bringing the best out in others. She loves generating insights and conversations helping make new connections in the brain and ultimately new social connections. Your world grows larger with every person that you meet.

Kerrie Phipps has written for regional and national magazines since 2006 and published her first book, *Create the Life Journal* in December 2008. One year later, Kerrie released *Lifting the Lid on Quiet Achievers – Success Stories of Regional Entrepreneurs*, which highlights success in regional Australia. *DO Talk To Strangers – How To Connect With Anyone, Anywhere* was inspired by the many people Kerrie connects with as she travels through life.

CONNECT WITH KERRIE

ASKING Kerrie to connect with you and your organisation...

We are all wired to connect; the idea of Connecting with Confidence these days is more likely to be associated with a secure Wi-Fi than making a meaningful connection with people around you. But in the world of Kerrie Phipps, Connecting with Confidence is the message she brings to people around the world. Smile, take a breath and say hello. Sometimes that's all you need.

Her book *DO Talk To Strangers – How To Connect With Anyone, Anywhere* was inspired by the many people Kerrie connects with as she travels through life. With the ASKING model she shares her experiences, and her six essential skills to more effectively engage and connect with others.

Kerrie is the kind of person who feels the fear and does it anyway, and in this book she shares her philosophy around contribution – which is more than just giving. Contribution is about adding value, and making the world a little better one connection at a time. ASKING looks at how to build AWARENESS, START small, KEEP going, be INTERESTED in others, tap into your NATURAL CONFIDENCE and finally to show GRATITUDE.

Kerrie has a simple message: Your world grows larger with every person you meet. In her keynotes and workshops, she helps people in customer-facing industries let go of the need to sell, and engage with the desire to connect.

The message from recent cognitive neuroscience research clearly shows that we are wired to connect. We achieve more in groups than alone; we create more; we stretch more; we contribute more. And yet, many of us resist connecting with others through fear, busyness, or sometimes plain old apathy.

To ignite this inbuilt desire to connect with others, invite Kerrie along to your organisation. At home as much in a boardroom as she is on stage, where there's an opportunity to encourage others and inspire them to connect more profoundly with those around them, ASKING is the key.

Described as having 'incredible energy on stage' Kerrie authentically models and teaches context-specific ways to connect with confidence both inside and outside the workplace. As a keynote speaker and conference culture specialist, Kerrie excels in bringing the best out in others.

Kerrie loves generating insights and conversations leading to new connections in the brain and ultimately new social connections. By ASKING Kerrie to speak with your team, you pave the way for new connections and business growth as she encourages others to:

- Connect more deeply with existing customers
- Confidently engage with new clients
- Contribute more to personal and business growth

Contact us today

Phone   +61 409 982 342
Enquiries   bookings@kerriephipps.com
Website   www.kerriephipps.com

Continue learning and sharing

Website

Visit www.kerriephipps.com to discover more valuable resources and register to keep connecting with anyone, anywhere. Access videos, audios, articles plus more!

Social Media

Facebook Page   kerriephipps1
Twitter   @kerriephipps
Instagram   @kerriephipps

tip

Connect - *Remember to connect well online; keep it personal by including a note or a question (to demonstrate you're a real person)* ☺

THANK YOU *Kerrie*

Ingram Content Group UK Ltd.
Milton Keynes UK
UKHW041407020623
422780UK00004B/374